AV·8 Harrier

James Wogstad and Jay Miller

With a special modeling section by Phil Friddell

Credits

Any monograph of this scope owes a great debt to many people. It would be impossible to list all of those persons who helped us; nevertheless we want to try . . .

Major Paul Chapman, who really got this project underway, and Major DeForest, both of PAO, Hq USMC;

Robert Carlisle, Head of Photojournalism and Public Inquiries Branch, OI, USN for the usual great selection of fine photographs;

Barry New, A.J. Geraghty and Teresa Mercill of Rolls Royce, Inc. for reams of background data and some especially fine photos;

John Glendinning and Doug Nelms of British Aerospace, Washington, D.C. and the Public Relations Department of British Aerospace, UK, for many excellent photographs;

Bert Cooper of the Congressional Research Service for some terrific background and historical material;

Capt. H.M. Snyder, Major L.M. Ricker and GSGT Rodrigues, USMC, Cherry Point MCAS for some very special photos of the TAV-8A;

Lt. Gen. Tom H. Miller, USMC (Ret.) for proofreading our manuscript, and consenting to do an interview . . . and Jack Elliott (AEROPHILE Associate Editor) for conducting the interview;

Major Paul Kahl and Lt. Col. Nick Apple, AFSINC, Hq, USAF for XV-6A photos;

The staff of the Marine Corps Still Photo Archives, History and Museums Division for many excellent AV-8A and TAV-8A photos;

Ted Bear, Edwards AFB Historian, for some good photographs of XV-6A testing at Edwards;

Al Frascella (PAO), Col. Stan Lewis (AV-8 Project Manager), Lt. Col. Jim Lary, Barry Berisfort and Major Brian O'Conner — all of Naval Air Systems Command for technical data;

Doree Martin of McDonnell Aircraft Company for technical data and photographs of AV-8B;

Brian Welch and Maurice Parker, PIO, at Langley Research Center for help with the XV-6A program;

Test Pilots Jack Reeder and Richard Culpepper, NASA Langley, for their technical assistance; and Bob Schade, for data on VIFF-ing;

Bill Frierson (PAO), and Don House (Flight Systems) at Pax River for some especially useful data and photographs of the early Kestrel tests;

Bill Schoeneberger (ex of Northrop) and Jim Corfield of Northrop Aviation for background information;

MSGT Bob Jarvis (PIO) Bergstrom AFB for his assistance ;

Derek Monk for his expertise and the loan of some good XV-6 material;

Harry Gann, John Kerr, Fred Harl, Hugh Alcock, Don Garrett, and Lon Nordeen for photographs; and Hal Andrews.

Last, but not least, thanks to Phil Friddell for preparing the section on modeling the Harrier.

For anyone we might have missed — we apologize. Please know that your contributions were appreciated.

The Authors

Published by Aerophile, Inc.
4014 Belle Grove, San Antonio, Texas 78230
Copyright © 1982 Aerophile, Inc.

Typeset and printed in the United States by San Antonio American Printers, San Antonio, Texas.

ISSN 0148-6691
ISBN 0-938664-00-X

FRONT COVER
Beautiful landing approach shot shows VMA-231 AV-8A in hover as it nears carrier deck for touchdown. *Rolls Royce photo*

BACK COVER
Prototype AV-8C CILOP conversion approaches the deck of the *U.S.S. Saipan* (LHA-2) during sea trials. *McDonnell Douglas photo.*

First flight of the advanced Harrier took place November 5, 1981 with McDonnell Douglas test pilot Charley Plummer at the controls. *McDonnell Douglas photo C12-11328-87*

Prototype AV-8C (BuNo. 158384) front view shows deployed air dam between gun canoes, revised wing pylons, and pattern of exhaust gasses as they exit nozzles during VTOL mode. *McDonnell Douglas photo*

View of prototype AV-8B during first test hop. *McDonnell Douglas photo*

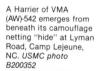

A Harrier of VMA (AW)-542 emerges from beneath its camouflage netting "hide" at Lyman Road, Camp Lejeune, NC. *USMC photo B200352*

2

Contents

AV-8A (BuNo: 158385) sits patiently while securely attached to elevator of *USS Guam (LPH-9)* during 1972 exercises in the Atlantic Ocean. *U.S. Navy photo K-95060 by D.L. Groner*

Kestrel XS691 hovers during Tripartite testing. This aircraft was later acquired by the United States as XV-6A, 64-18265. *Hawker Siddeley photo 68726*

TAV-8A (BuNo. 159378) demonstrates its low altitude hover capability during early Marine Corps acceptance trials in England. *Rolls Royce photo E 201328*

3

Forward

Man has striven and always will strive for progress and improvement in his existing environment. The rate of success in his ventures is generally limited by at least two major factors. First, he must overcome the problems of nature, the unknown, and/or physics; and second, he must overcome the lack of support or even the hindrance or obstructive effort placed on him by his fellow man, the non-believer, and those with conflicting self-interests.

The successful development of vertical and/or short takeoff and landing (V/STOL) high-performance aircraft has followed along these traditional restraints. From the mid-1950's, until the beginning of the 1970's, the limitations to V/STOL progress were primarily those of overcoming problems of nature. Fortunately for those of us here in the United States, our friends in the United Kingdom attacked these problems with tenacity and a stubborn refusal to give up that is so characteristic of the English. As a result, the breakthrough to successful military high performance V/STOL operationally suitable and feasible aircraft came in the late 1960's. It was at this point that the United States began to receive some return on its rather meager support to the United Kingdom's efforts and its own many failures.

This return on investment came as a result of the U.S. Marine Corps efforts to satisfy a vital and urgently needed system that would provide a significant improvement on the battlefield. This improvement would be the saving of many Marines' lives while in combat and would add significantly to the probability of their success in battle.

Throughout the 1970's the Marine Corps operated the Harrier with great success, proving beyond doubt that high-performance V/STOL aircraft are as vital to military operations as the helicopter, the tank, and the ships at sea. Yet, even today in the United States, progress has been significantly slowed because of the disruptive efforts of a few high-placed individuals who either refuse to take the time to acquaint themselves with the facts of performance and tactics, or are driven by conflicting self-interests.

I applaud the efforts of the authors of this book for the depth of research that it has taken to bring the facts to the readers. As in any account such as this, it is very difficult to be letter perfect; however, this particular AV-8 history is certainly the most unbiased and factual account yet compiled. The reader will undoubtedly be far better informed and stimulated into wondering why so much time has been wasted toward progress of a system that has proven it's success to a degree higher than many of man's improvements in the aeronautical field.

Thomas H. Miller
Lt. General, U.S. Marine Corps
(Retired)

AV-8A launches from deck of *USS Guam* (LPH-9) during interim sea control tests in the Atlantic Ocean. *U.S. Navy photo 1151426 by C.V. Sneed*

VMAT-203 TAV-8A makes "ski jump" takeoff from special ramp during April 1979 tests. Ski jump improves STOL performance of AV-8 by a substantial margin and will likely become a standard feature of ships designed to accomodate the AV-8. *McDonnell Douglas photo C12-7593-1*

Introduction

BIRTH OF A CONCEPT

The development of successful and efficient vertical takeoff and landing (VTOL) aircraft has long been a dream of aircraft designers. From da Vinci to the present, the requirement for vertical takeoff and landing capability has remained constant.

Historically, the major hindrance to successful VTOL has been the classic problem of power-to-weight ratio. Simply stated, it has been only during the course of the past quarter century that powerplants capable of producing the amount of energy necessary for VTOL operation have become available. True day-to-day operational capability can claim an even more recent birthdate.

Unquestionably the first production fixed-wing aircraft in the world to benefit from this advanced VTOL engine technology is the Hawker Harrier. Originally developed for use by Britain's Royal Air Force and Royal Navy, the type has grown significantly in popularity. Today it equips the United States Marine Corps and Spanish Navy, and has received strong consideration by a number of other foreign military services (including that of the People's Republic of China). Its future, particularly in consideration of the fact that new, improved, and advanced configurations remain either in production or under development, is particularly bright. The Harrier will likely see front line service in one variant or another until well into the early twenty-first century.

Low-angle three-quarter front view of XV-6A. Nozzle angle is not quite 90-degrees to centerline. Hover is usually accomplished in this slightly nose high attitude. *NASA*

Similar in appearance to the AV-8A beyond, the Harrier II is characterized by its raised cockpit, bubble canopy, longer fuselage, and lift improvement devices. *McDonnell Douglas photo C22-282-14*

Number 2 aircraft of the Tri-Service test squadron is shown during shipboard trials in May, 1966. View is from a stern position, looking forward across the minimal flight deck to the superstructure of the *U.S.S. Raleigh* (LPD-1). *U.S. Navy photo courtesy of Hal Andrews*

Engine EVOLUTION

The story of the United States Marine Corps use and further development of Britain's Hawker Harrier began with the birth of the original Hawker VTOL program in early 1957. Interestingly, the birth of the airframe actually took place after the birth of the powerplant; which, in turn, followed the development of a practical means of thrust vectoring.

The vectoring of the thrust of a jet engine was first propounded for a practical aircraft by Monsieur Michel Wibault (who was, incidentally, the noteworthy designer of a number of successful French military aircraft). After being refused assistance by the French government, Wibault submitted, in 1956, a proposal for a ''ground attack gyrocopter'' with STOL (Short Takeoff and Landing) capabilities to Sir Alec Coryton and Dr. Stanley Hooker of Britain's Bristol Aero Engines.

Wibault's proposal consisted of an 8,000 hp Bristol Orion turboprop driving four centrifugal ''blowers'', the casings of which could be rotated to direct the compressed air, and hence the reaction, or thrust, through 90-degrees. Though this arrangement was too heavy and cumbersome to be a really practical proposition, it embodied the two fundamental features of the future Harrier engine, the Pegasus — full rotatable thrust, and a thrust resultant acting near the aircraft's center of gravity.

Using Wibault's basic idea, the next step was to lighten and simplify the design. To begin with, the four centrifugal blowers were replaced by an axial-flow fan with two rotatable nozzles. This layout, eventually designated BE48 by Bristol, retained the Orion reduction gear to drive the fan, thus still incurring a considerable weight penalty. It was then decided to drive it by means of a ''free'' turbine running at the required speed.

This was not possible with the Orion, since it already had two concentric shaft systems, so the single-shaft, lightweight Orpheus turbojet was investigated and shown to give adequate performance with a 60-percent weight saving. The resulting design, the BE52, was soon developed into the BE53, which consisted of an Orpheus gas generator plus three stages of an Olympus LP (Low Pressure) compressor driven by a separate two-stage turbine. The Orpheus compressor shaft was large enough for the shaft driving the fan to run inside it — the shafts rotating in opposite directions to minimize gyroscopic effects. The relatively cool fan air was discharged through two swivelling nozzles while the gas generator efflux was discharged through a conventional jet pipe at the rear.

The BE53 was never to reach production, though a follow-on development, the BE53/2 would, as the Pegasus 1. The conventional jet pipe of the BE53 was replaced by a bifurcated duct with another pair of swivelling nozzles, giving the now familiar four-nozzle layout, and the fan was redesigned as an overhung unit with two rotating stages. The Pegasus 1 first ran in September of 1959, producing 9,000 pounds of thrust.

The Pegasus 2, a logical follow-on to the Pegasus 1, was a revision of the Pegasus 1 design following the decision to use compressor delivery air for aircraft stabilization. This necessitated increasing the HP (High Pressure) airflow capacity — achieved by replacing the Orpheus 3 compressor with an Orpheus 6 unit, which was dimensionally similar. The engine, in its new form, ran on the bench for the first time in February of 1960, and was cleared for flight initially at 11,000 and subsequently 12,000 pounds thrust with a life (time between overhauls) of 15 hours in VTOL and 20 hours in conventional flight.

This powerplant was installed in the prototype Hawker P.1127 and powered the aircraft during its historic first tethered hover in October of 1960. It was also the powerplant that allowed the first P.1127 transition from vertical to horizontal flight the following September.

Airframe EVOLUTION

During the course of this extensive engine development program, Hawker had been forging ahead with the design of their proposed VTOL testbed airframe. In fact, shortly after Wibault first contacted Coryton and Hooker at Bristol, Hooker had carried the idea to the British Ministry of Supply and to Sir Sidney Camm, Hawker Aircraft's famous technical director.

Camm, interestingly enough, had already devoted a number of years to the study of jet lift and had received official support for a proposed jet lift testbed tentatively referred to as the P.1127. This project had been stalled, however, by inherent powerplant and hover stability problems and had been placed on the back burner until solutions could be developed.

By the time the Pegasus 1 had reached an initial stage of maturity in mid-1957, Hawker and Camm felt that they were ready to proceed with the development and full-scale construction of the P.1127 airframe. Unfortunately, the timing of these respective declarations of confidence was extraordinarily bad. For it was at just this point in British defense procurement that the British Minister of

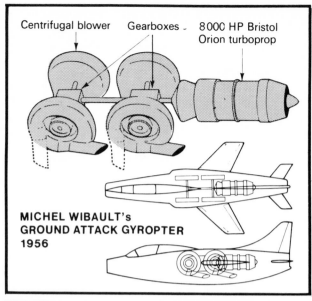

MICHEL WIBAULT's GROUND ATTACK GYROPTER 1956

Centrifugal blower   Gearboxes   8000 HP Bristol Orion turboprop

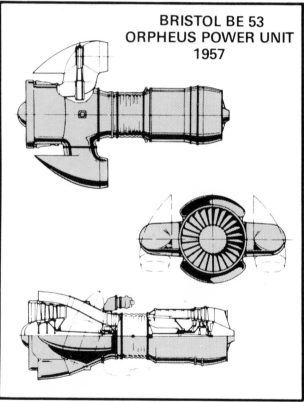

BRISTOL BE 53 ORPHEUS POWER UNIT 1957

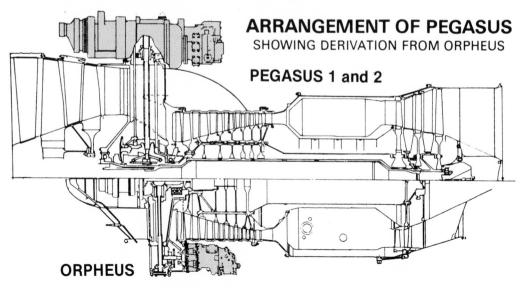

ARRANGEMENT OF PEGASUS
SHOWING DERIVATION FROM ORPHEUS

PEGASUS 1 and 2

ORPHEUS

Defense declared, in his infamous Defense White Paper, that the Royal Air Force would not likely be acquiring any further manned aircraft beyond those already on order.

The burden of proof of concept now lay on the shoulders of Hawker. Without government funding, it would take substantial company money to keep the project afloat through prototype development and flight test.

The directors of Hawker were not long in reaching a decision. Not surprisingly, they expressed strong belief in Camm's VTOL project (which, as point of interest, was also the end result of work done by Camm's engineering associates, John Fozard and Ralph Hooper) and agreed to arrange in-house funding if additional monies could be gotten from NATO's American-funded Mutual Weapons Development Program (MWDP) for powerplant development. Accordingly, Hawker and Bristol representatives went to Paris to meet with NATO MWDP personnel.

As it were, NATO had been supporting a new, light tactical strike fighter program under MWDP for some time. Thanks to good timing, the Hawker and Bristol team managed to convince the MWDP representatives that the proposed British VTOL aircraft could be developed specifically to meet the needs of this role and that it should be looked at in terms of a lengthy exploratory project.

Following the meeting, the MWDP people agreed to furnish some seventy-five percent of the requested BE53 funding — with Hawker and Bristol

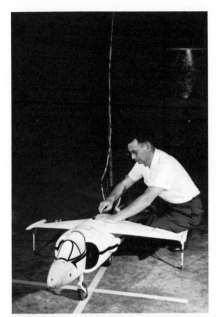

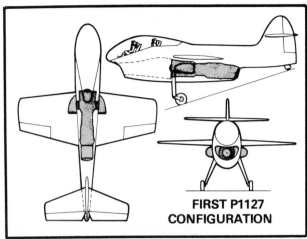

Flyable and controllable scale model of the P.1127 was built for tunnel testing at NASA Langley. Model was used to verify many of the flight and hover characteristics of the P.1127 design. NASA, in turn, gained significant experience in the design of vectored thrust VTOL aircraft. *NASA photo L-60-2544 and NASA photo L-60-1145*

FIRST P1127 CONFIGURATION

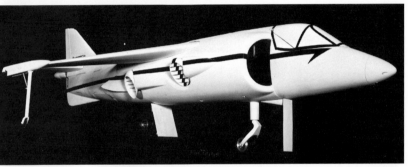

Four views illustrate early wind tunnel tests of Harrier and Kestrel configurations. Note that photo in upper left shows Harrier mounting four free-falling conventional weapons, and Harrier in lower right mounts two anti-ship missiles. *Rolls Royce photo E223926*

putting up the remaining twenty-five percent. At the same time, NATO put together a new specification for a jet V/STOL replacement for the limited capability Fiat G.91 — thus giving the proposed VTOL aircraft a reason to exist.

By mid-1958, Hawker had elected to proceed with the development of two P.1127 prototypes. During the preceeding twelve months, much preliminary development and design work had taken place, this including a basic reorientation of the project to fulfill the requirements of the NATO light tactical strike fighter program.

Engine development had proceeded at a rapid pace also, and by the time Hawker was ready to commit itself to the airframe hardware stage, Bristol was ready to forge ahead with an 11,000 pound thrust derivative of the Pegasus 1. This new engine was considered the minimal powerplant necessary to get the envisioned airframe and one-man crew off the ground.

Much research and development work had already been accomplished by the time the first metal was cut in late 1959. Scale models, for instance, had revealed a number of phenomenon unique to the vectored thrust VTOL configuration, not the least of which was exhaust patterns that caused problems with reingestion of exhaust gasses. Another phenomenon was the discovery that exhaust flows from the engine would, when the airplane was in ground effect, reflect back off the ground and impinge upon its underside, thus increasing the engine's effective lift thrust by a substantial margin.

A problem of some import that was not long in being solved was that of airplane control in low or zero speed flight conditions. The eventual solution was to equip the airplane with reaction control jets in the nose, tail, and wingtips. These were basically valves mounted at the end of pipes which served to transfer high pressure (and high temperature) bleed air from the engine's forward compressor section to the respective c.g. moment-arm points on the airframe.

Additional work also covered the development of the lightweight, bicycle type main landing gear and its associated outriggers. Mounted centrally on the fuselage, this gear allowed the inclusion of the vectored thrust engine configuration and at the same time, provided an extremely stable platform in ground taxi, conventional takeoff, and conventional landing.

Work on VTOL aircraft in the United States also played a significant role in the development of the P.1127. Bell Aerospace Textron (in 1957, still known as Bell Aircraft Corporation) had, earlier in the decade, initiated work on a large number of VTOL designs that had culminated in the actual construction of two testbed aircraft. These were the Bell ATV (also referred to as the Bell VTOL) and the Bell X-14.

The latter project and associated flight test program proved of significant interest to Hawker's design and flight test team, and in 1960 arrangements were made with the X-14's operating agency (NASA) for the team to examine and fly it. Hawker's chief test pilot, Bill Bedford, flew the X-14 on a number of occcasions during visits to NASA's Ames Research Center in California.

It was in December of 1959 that the British government at last elected to express official interest in the P.1127 program by supporting it under a research funding arrangement entitled Experimental Requirement E.R. 204D. In a related development, Operational Requirement O.R. 345 was also tendered, this effectively opening the way for a potential production order for an operational variant.

U.S. interest in the Hawker VTOL strike fighter was more than just passing. Much preliminary wind tunnel work was conducted in 1959 at various facilities around the U.S., including NASA Langley. The results of this work played a significant role in the final design of the airplane and, as we shall see, in the decision to buy the airplane for U.S. military use.

By the spring of 1960, the two prototype P.1127's and the one structural test airframe were well along in construction. All of this activity, it must be emphasized, was still taking place financed almost totally in-house by Hawker. It wasn't until June of 1960 that the actual contract with the British Government was signed for prototypes XP831 and XP836.

June also saw delivery of the first Pegasus 2 engine for installation in the first Hawker airframe. By now the engine was considered developed enough to safely allow initiation of preliminary flight tests, though time between overhaul (TBO) was less than 20 hours for hovering flight.

Hawker had also initiated discussions calling for the construction of an additional four prototypes (XP972, XP975, XP980, and XP984). Problems arose concerning funding, however, and a decision on this proposal was postponed until the first two prototypes could prove the project's viability.

The prototype P.1127, XP831, was rolled from Hawker's Dunsfold facility in late July of 1960, and the following month began tie-down tests over a specially designed (and specially built) pit with metal grate. The latter permitted a variety of tests to be conducted and avoided problems with foreign object ingestion, excessive noise, and exhaust reingestion.

Flight Tests BEGIN

The first true hover, with Hawker test pilot Bill Bedford at the controls, took place on October 21st in a tethered state. An altitude of some two feet was achieved without problems.

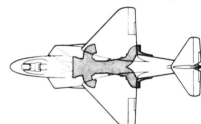

P.1127 prototype hovers over test pit during early tethered trials. Note extended intake lip for improved intake efficiency at zero forward speeds. Also note fixed boundary layer splitter plate. In this photo, pitot boom has yet to be attached, balancing wheels are not covered by normal fairings, and main gear doors are not attached. This airplane is the father of all Kestrel's and Harrier's. *Hawker Siddeley photo EXP 343/60*

REVISED P1127 CONFIGURATION

By this time, the Pegasus 2 was producing just over 11,000 pounds thrust. On November 19th, following additional over-pit hovering flights, the tethers were removed and the airplane was "walked" by its pilot to solid ground and landed — thus successfully completing the first free hover of the program.

Once these initial hover trials were successfully concluded, the airplane was given its preliminary taxi tests, again at Dunsford. Unfortunately, the length of the runway, coupled with other safety considerations, dictated that high-speed taxi trials and conventional flight tests be undertaken at another facility. Shortly afterwards, the airplane was transported by truck to the Royal Aeronautical Establishment (RAE) test facility at Bedford. There, high-speed taxi tests were undertaken and successfully completed, these being followed by the first conventional flight on March 13, 1961, again with Bill Bedford at the controls.

Following additional tests at Dunsfold, XP831 embarked on an extensive flight test program in concert with its newly completed stablemate, XP836. The latter airplane had flown for the first time in conventional fashion, on July 7th.

With both P.1127's now flying, exploration of the type's flight envelope was carried on at a rapid pace. XP831 explored the high speed segment of the envelope, and XP836 the low speed. By September 12th, almost all aspects of the performance capability of the design had been demonstrated, including vertical takeoffs, inflight translations, and vertical landings. Test pilot Bedford, incidentally, had been joined in the program by several other Hawker pilots, these including Hugh Merewether, Duncan Simpson, and John Farley.

December of 1961 proved a rather noteworthy month for the P.1127. Supersonic flight (in a shallow dive) was achieved for the first time; and XP836

crashed. The cause of the latter was quickly traced to loss of one of the fiberglass engine exhaust nozzles. Fortunately, Bedford, the pilot, successfully ejected at an altitude of about 250 feet. The airplane, however, was totally destroyed. A less fatigue-prone all-metal nozzle soon replaced the glass-fiber type.

Flight testing continued with XP831 and the first of the afore-mentioned four additional prototypes, XP972. The latter aircraft, at long last, had been approved for construction in late 1960 by the British Ministry of Supply.

XP972 was the first of the new batch to fly, this taking place on April 5, 1962. It was followed by XP975, XP980, and finally, XP984, which was delivered on February 24, 1963.

During the course of the P.1127 flight test program XP972 was lost in a non-fatal accident. Several months later, XP831 undertook the first shipboard deck trials aboard *H.M.S. Ark Royal* in the English Channel and, several months after that, the type made its first appearance at the Paris Air Show. Unfortunately, during a demonstration, it crashed, though without injury to the pilot.

It should be noted that each of the first six P.1127's differed significantly one from the other. The first two prototypes, though externally similar, were quite dissimilar internally, having different engine modifications, different avionics systems, and different miscellaneous subsystems. XP975 incorporated an interim wing with a stability-improving kinked leading edge; XP980 introduced an enlarged slab stabilator with greatly increased anhedral; XP972 (and XP980) tested the new drag reducing "Kuchemann"-type wingtip; and XP984 introduced and tested an almost totally new wing that was swept on both the leading and trailing edges.

As with all testbed aircraft, the six prototypes underwent a wide variety of

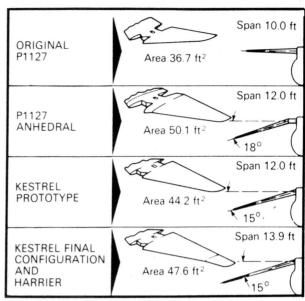

TAILPLANE DEVELOPMENT

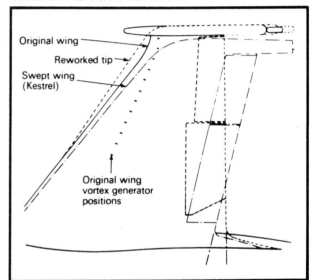

WING GEOMETRY DEVELOPMENT

Unusual shot showing four of the tri-partite P.1127 Kestrel's in flight together. Aircraft in photo include XS689 (#9), XS691 (#1), XS694 (#4), and XS695 (#5). *British Aerospace photo*

modifications and updates during the courses of their respective lives. Not only did these modifications improve performance and handling, they also represented baseline criteria for the development of new and much improved production configurations.

Phase I testing of the P.1127's continued throughout the summer of 1961. By September 20, it had been convincingly concluded. Advanced testing was now undertaken.

Tripartite PROGRAM

In January of 1962, plans were officially announced by the British Government for creation of a "tripartite" P.1127 program involving Britain, the United States, and West Germany. This program would consist of a multinational evaluation squadron to be equipped solely with P.1127's. It was born out of the strong interest in the P.1127 expressed by the U.S. and Germany, and the British government's sudden realization that this strange little airplane, with its unique VTOL capabilities, just might have some tactical use as well as foreign sales potential.

The U.S. interest in the tripartite program had not been of recent vintage. As mentioned earlier, NASA Langley's wind tunnel facilities had played a significant role in the early development of the basic design, and Bell's X-14 had been used to introduce Hawker test pilots Bill Bedford and Hugh Merewether to the peculiarities of VTOL flight. In June of 1962, two NASA test pilots, Jack Reeder and Fred Drinkwater, flew one of the prototype P.1127's, making suggestions that shortly afterwards led to the addition of an increase in vertical fin area — which has since become a standard fixture on the type.

The fundamental objective of the tripartite evaluation squadron effort was to determine how best to operate VTOL-capable aircraft in an operational environment. As VTOL performance had never before been available for service test evaluation, the work of the tripartite squadron was considered particularly important. Criteria born out of its activities would likely serve as VTOL aircraft operating standards for many years to come.

Overseen by a policy committee and management board and directly controlled by a Joint Military Evaluation Group, the tripartite squadron effort was officially consumated on February 20, 1962. By the time the unit became officially ready for trials (as No. 38 Group, RAF Transport Command), it consisted of the following pilots: Wg. Cdr. David McL. Scrimgeour (RAF); Sqn. Ldr. F.A. Trowern (RAF); Flt. Lt. R.J.A. Munro (RAF); Flt. Lt. David J. McL. Edmondston (RAF); Col. G.F. Barkhorn (Luft.); 1st Lt. V. Suhr (Luft.); Cdr. J.J. Tyson, Jr. (USN); Maj. J.K. Campbell (USAF); Maj. J.A. Johnston (US Army); and Lt. Col. L.K. Solt (later replaced by Maj. P.R. Curry) (US Army).

Administrative and maintenance personnel participating totalled at an additional 35 from the U.S., 41 from Great Britain, and 36 from Germany. Among the former were scientific and technical advisors, as well as a small collection of photographers and data recording specialists.

The decision to create the tripartite evaluation squadron also gave birth to a much improved version of the basic P.1127 called the Kestrel whose namesake, an Old World falcon, is particularly noted for its hovering/gliding hunting technique. Ordered by the British Military of Aviation on May 21, 1962, this airplane was an evolutionary development of its predecessor (the P.1127) and differed from it considerably. Of perhaps paramount importance was the fact that it was powered by the significantly more powerful Pegasus 5. Rated at over 15,200 pounds thrust, this engine incorporated a new three-stage fan with no inlet guide vanes (it had, instead, guide vanes added to the front of the compressor section). The cannular combustion chamber was replaced with a fully annular unit and the first stage high-pressure turbine rotor blades were air-cooled. The Pegasus 5 had first run in June of 1962 and was to enter limited production and limited service with the advent of the Kestrel tripartite evaluation squadron in April of 1965.

Nine aircraft (and 18 engines) were involved in the Kestrel production run, these including XS688, XS689, XS690, XS691, XS692, XS693, XS694, XS695, and XS696. All made their first flights during a twelve month period between March of 1964 and March of 1965. It is of some import to note that XP984, one of the original P.1127's, was modified to Kestrel standards and, in fact, served as the Kestrel prototype.

Besides the afore-mentioned engine improvements, the Kestrel differed from the P.1127 in having an improved wing with tapering sweep, broader chord, more area, and revised wingtips. It also incorporated anhedral in the slab stabilator, a longer fuselage with improved fineness ratio, and more internal volume to accommodate the Pegasus 5 dimensional requirements. Last but not least, it incorporated a much improved intake design with a fixed geometry lip and throat (the prototype

Two of the tri-partite squadron P.1127 Kestrel's, XS694 and XS695 hover during British field service tests. XS694 eventually became NASA 520 and crashed at Wallops Island, Virginia in late 1967. XS695 remained in England as part of Hawker Siddeley/Royal Air Force Harrier test unit. *NASA photo L-71-3607*

Airborne shot of XS688 showing tri-partite markings (mirrored images in this photo — they were later changed to same design for both wings). *British Aerospace photo P1127-146/64*

Photo of first tri-partite P.1127, XS688, during early flight test trials. Note that this airplane is mounting external fuel tanks under wing — somewhat unusual at this time due to early stage of flight test. Note also, the rubberized intake lip. *British Aerospace photo 1127 (R)265/64*

P.1127's had gone through a number of intake designs, including one that consisted of an inflatable rubberized lip — inflation taking place at low speeds and supposedly providing improved airflow to the face of the engine compressor section). In total, the Kestrel was a virtually new airplane. There were few parts interchangeable between it and the original P.1127's.

The tripartite squadron officially formed on October 15, 1964. Following introductory instruction for the maintenance crews at Hawker's facility at Dunsfold, and a slightly shorter introductory course for pilots (one week of ground school and three hours of flight conversion), the unit set up a base of operations at West Raynham near Fakenham, Norfolk, England. This site proved ideal because it was near a number of unused airfields and offered a number of other challenges particularly suitable to the program's VTOL capability.

It should be noted that the conversion of the tripartite program pilots created few problems. The average conversion took 10 sorties; about 11 vertical takeoffs and landings, about 11 short takeoffs and landings, 3 conventional takeoffs and landings, and 5 accelerating and decelerating transitions. Another 13 flights in the airplane were completed by each pilot by the time the tripartite

operations actually got underway.

Several basic tasks were set aside as tripartite squadron objectives. These included (1) exploration of flight operating procedures and techniques; (2) comparison of various takeoff and landing modes and techniques; (3) exploration of jet-borne operations in low-speed flight; (4) V/STOL aircraft field suitability in an operational environment; (5) instrument flying; and (6) night flying.

U.S. involvement in the tripartite evaluation squadron had begun in December of 1961. Following the initiative of the West German government (which had signed a bilateral development agreement with England several months earlier), the U.S. had proposed that it be allowed to join the British/German consortium and share the P.1127's associated development costs. Born at this same time was the tripartite evaluation squadron idea . . ., which, interestingly enough, was American in origin.

In truth, the U.S. had maintained more than a passing interest in the P.1127's development for a number of years. The U.S. Army, in 1962, had been impressed with early reports of P.1127 capabilities and had shown such a strong interest that the Northrop Corporation had met with Hawker and agreed to a collaborative deal whereby the two firms

KESTREL JET REACTION CONTROL SYSTEM

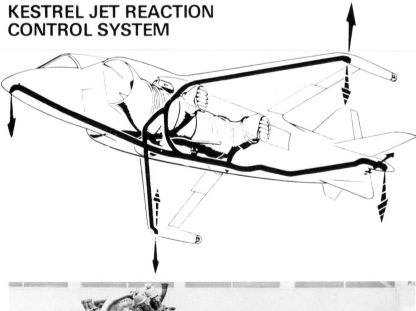

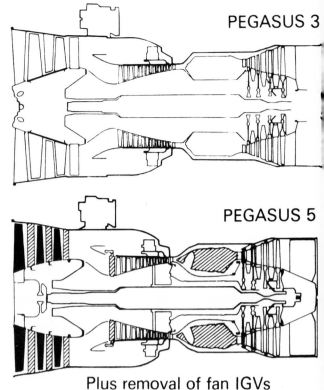

PEGASUS 3

PEGASUS 5

Plus removal of fan IGVs

PEGASUS 6

Plus 2-vane nozzles

PEGASUS 11

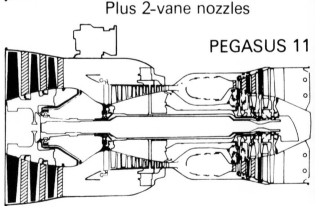

Plus revised fuel system improved water injection

PEGASUS TYPE DIFFERENCES

Minus forward exhaust nozzles, an XV-6A Rolls Royce Pegasus engine sits on its dolly at NASA Langley. Note immense rubber support cushions underneath engine support bracket. *NASA photo L-67-6308*

would share VTOL information (though one might ask what Northrop could offer!). Part of this arrangement apparently included P.1127 manufacturing rights for Northrop.

Thanks to a slowly maturing governmental belief in VTOL machines, it was announced by then-Secretary of Defense Robert McNamara that the U.S. would contribute $30 to $35-million towards the development of the P.1127 and its engine. This was followed by the Drinkwater/Reeder pilot evaluation at Dunsfold, already mentioned.

Following an abbreviated test and development program, the Kestrel, in December of 1964, was released by the British government for full service evaluation and use. This was the first such event in the history of fixed-wing VTOL aircraft — not only for Britain, but for the world.

The original U.S. tripartite proposal had called for the limited production of 18 evaluation aircraft with six being assigned to each participating country. However, due to the limited amount of money available, only nine aircraft were eventually procured — with each country being assigned 3. It was also decided that each country, at the end of the program, would be given the option of buying its three aircraft.

Following the official founding at West Raynham, the tripartite squadron began its flight program on April 1, 1965. During the following eleven months, 938 takeoffs and 600 flight hours were logged. One airplane was lost early in the program because of a minor pilot error (the pilot escaped unharmed).

The evaluation involved every possible contingency a VTOL attack aircraft might encounter in actual combat. All types of terrain were investigated for purposes of determining which made the best surfaces for VTOL operations; and a variety of weather conditions were tackled with similar zeal.

Throughout the evaluation program no live armament was carried aboard the aircraft. In fact, the only armament-related equipment to be found was a rudimentary visual gunsight mounted over the instrument panel combing. Pilots could only pretend to attack surface and air-to-air targets (effectivity of the aircraft as a weapons carrier therefore remained somewhat in question.)

Many problems were encountered and overcome during the course of the Kestrel trials. Surprisingly, the airplane's maintainability proved quite good, especially in consideration of the fact that both the airframe and the engine

were virtually untested at the time the tripartite evaluation squadron was formed.

Due to the Kestrel's unique exhaust pattern, some concern had been expressed over problems with surface

XV-6A (64-18266) lifts off from the *U.S.S. Raleigh* (LPD-1) during Kestrel sea trials in May, 1966. *U.S. Navy photo 1115757*

XV-6A, 64-18264 (#4) in U.S. Air Force markings, Edwards AFB, California, October 1967. Markings were essentially the same as for the tri-service evaluation except for the addition of "U.S. Air Force" above forward nozzle; "USAF" on upper right and lower left wings; and the deletion of the Tri-Service tail band.

Nose boom is half white, and striped red and natural metal. Of all the XV-6As assigned to Edwards AFB (Numbers 2, 4, 5 and 6) only 64-18265

and 64-18266 had fuselage insignia applied. Additionally a red turbine warning stripe was applied just aft of the forward nozzles.

XV-6A, 64-18262 (#2) in U.S. Tri-Service Evaluation markings. Shipboard evaluation aboard the *U.S.S. Independence*, May, 1966. Aircraft is overall natural metal with black serials, nose numbers and individual markings.

64-18262 (#2) Dice
64-18263 (#3) Question Mark
64-18264 (#4) no marking
64-18265 (#5) Cyclops
64-18266 (#6) Wolfhead
64-18267 (#7) Bat
Tri-Service tail band was white, edged red with black lettering. National insignia appears only on upper left and lower right wing. Nose numbers were the last digits of the serial numbers. Forward nozzle antenna were black.

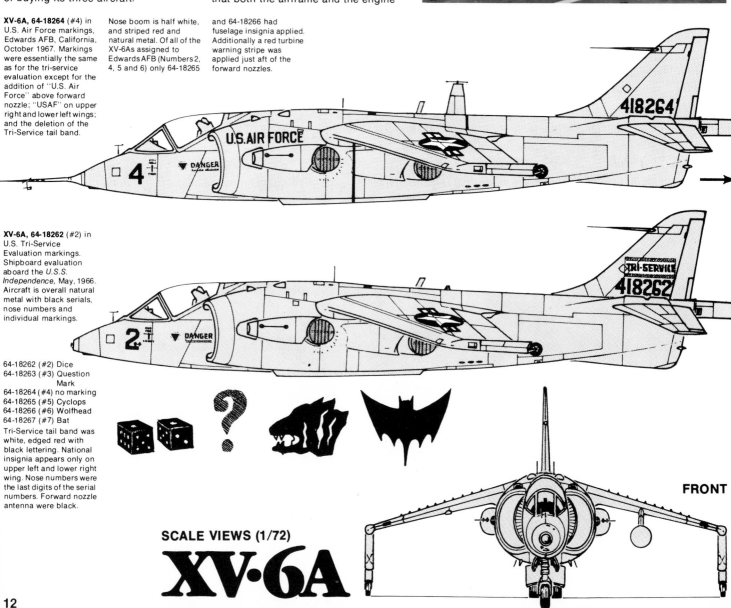

SCALE VIEWS (1/72)

XV·6A

FRONT

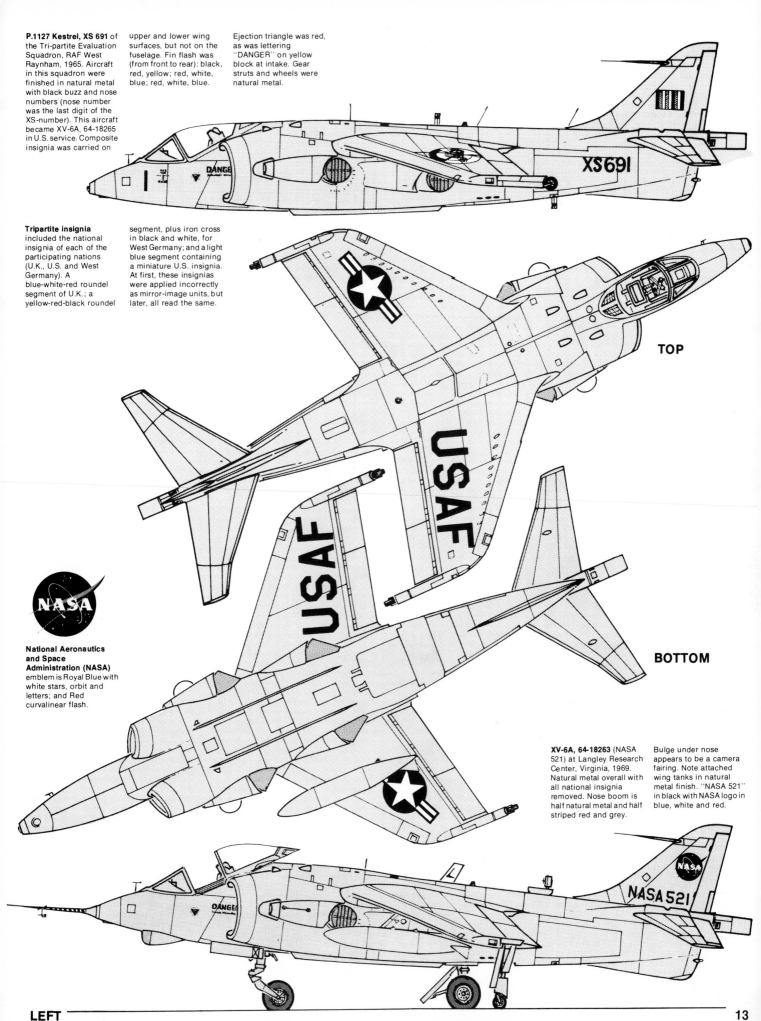

P.1127 Kestrel, XS 691 of the Tri-partite Evaluation Squadron, RAF West Raynham, 1965. Aircraft in this squadron were finished in natural metal with black buzz and nose numbers (nose number was the last digit of the XS-number). This aircraft became XV-6A, 64-18265 in U.S. service. Composite insignia was carried on upper and lower wing surfaces, but not on the fuselage. Fin flash was (from front to rear): black, red, yellow; red, white, blue; red, white, blue.

Ejection triangle was red, as was lettering "DANGER" on yellow block at intake. Gear struts and wheels were natural metal.

Tripartite insignia included the national insignia of each of the participating nations (U.K., U.S. and West Germany). A blue-white-red roundel segment of U.K.; a yellow-red-black roundel segment, plus iron cross in black and white, for West Germany; and a light blue segment containing a miniature U.S. insignia. At first, these insignias were applied incorrectly as mirror-image units, but later, all read the same.

National Aeronautics and Space Administration (NASA) emblem is Royal Blue with white stars, orbit and letters; and Red curvalinear flash.

TOP

BOTTOM

XV-6A, 64-18263 (NASA 521) at Langley Research Center, Virginia, 1969. Natural metal overall with all national insignia removed. Nose boom is half natural metal and half striped red and grey.

Bulge under nose appears to be a camera fairing. Note attached wing tanks in natural metal finish. "NASA 521" in black with NASA logo in blue, white and red.

erosion. It was known that, during hover, the exhaust efflux was of such strength that unsecured surfaces such as sand and snow would be blown into the air in such quantities that the potential for reingestion was great. Accordingly, much research was conducted in this area, eventually leading to the development of artificial surfaces and takeoff and landing pad criterion.

The end result of the tripartite squadron effort was proof that VTOL attack aircraft of the Kestrel type could safely and effectively operate away from front line bases with a minimal amount of logistical support and equipment. Additionally, it was proven beyond any shadow of a doubt that a VTOL attack aircraft was a feasible proposition, not only in terms of effectivity, but also from

a technical standpoint. Most importantly, it was demonstrated that no special pilot skills were required for safe and efficient flying.

U.S.Kestrel TESTS

Once the tripartite operation ended on November 30, 1965, the United States elected to accept the three aircraft it

Ships #2 and #7 in XV-6A fleet are shown on the line following their arrival, along with two sister ships, at Pax River, Maryland. The date is May 5, 1966. 418267 was unable to participate in the sea trials because of a damaged nose gear. U.S. Navy photo PAP-26153-5-66/NATC Patuxent River

Elevator lifts XV-6A (A.F. serial 64-18262) to deck level of carrier USS Independence (CVA-62). Note fuel truck in background. U.S. Navy photo via NATC Patuxent River

Detail of XV-6A forward exhaust nozzle and nose landing gear. Compare XV-6A gear to AV-8A production gear. The latter is substantially larger and heavier. U.S. Navy photo via NATC Patuxent River

XV-6A (A.F. serial 64-18264) wingtip balancing wheels are also slightly less substantial than those of the AV-8A production model. Note complex fairing design. Also note RAT in extended position. U.S. Navy photo via NATC Patuxent River

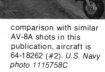

Excellent frontal view of one of the Tri-Service XV-6As aboard the U.S.S. Independence (CV-62) provides a good comparison with similar AV-8A shots in this publication, aircraft is 64-18262 (#2). U.S. Navy photo 1115758C

was operating as well as the three flown by the Federal Republic of Germany. The latter country had elected not to take up its acquisition option.

The six U.S. Kestrel aircraft were transported by ship, in early 1966, to the U.S. for tri-service testing. Once in the U.S. they were allocated the designation of XV-6A. Previous to this the

P.1127/Kestrel had been assigned other designations. These were:

VZ-12 . . . designation reserved for two P.1127 aircraft to be assigned serial numbers 62-4507/4508. These were not delivered and the numbers were assigned as part of a purchase of H-43Bs.

V-6 . . . redesignation of VZ-12. Six

P.1127 Kestrels for tri-service evaluation (64-18262/18267).

XV-6A was a redesignation of the V-6 purchase.

Shortly after their arrival, the six aircraft were transferred to the Army's Fort Campbell, Kentucky facility and there participated in a number of Army ground support related tests that took

This photo shows XV-6A trials on board USS *Raleigh* (LPD-1) in May 1966. *U.S. Navy photo 1115763*

Beautiful underside view of XV-6A (64-18263) in flight during Tri-Service testing. *U.S. Navy photo 1115755*

Preparing XV-6A (A.F. serial 64-18264) for launch during carrier qualification on board the carrier *USS Independence* (CVA-62). Note open

ended tail cone. It is likely that this normally contained an anti-spin parachute. *U.S. Navy photo via NATC Patuxent River*

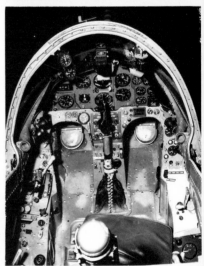

Good static shot of XV-6A (A.F. serial 64-18264) taken during carrier qualification trials aboard *USS Independence* (CVA-62) in May of 1966. Attitude ball in nose is readily apparent. *U.S. Navy photo via NATC Patuxent River*

Cockpit photo of XV-6A (A.F. serial 64-18263), NASA 521. This particular airplane is now permanently displayed as part of the National Air & Space Museum collection, Washington, D.C. *NASA photo L-72-373*

15

from late March to late-April for completion.

Once test program responsibility was turned over to the Navy, five aircraft were transferred from Fort Campbell to the Naval Air Test Center at Patuxent River NAS, Maryland where they were used in a series of land-based tests created to determine their effectiveness while operating from the decks of various types of U.S. Navy ships. Airplane 64-18267 suffered gear damage in a hard landing accident during these tests. This program lasted from May 3 to May 8, at which time a ferry flight of the four airworthy aircraft (2,3,4 and 6) to Norfolk NAS took place. From there, they were loaded aboard the *U.S.S. Independence* for initiation of preliminary sea trials.

The pilots for this latter undertaking consisted of Cdr. J.J. Tyson (USN); Maj. J.K. Campbell (USAF); Maj. P. Curry (U.S. Army); Maj. J.A. Johnston (US Army); and Col. G. Barkhorn (W. Ger. AF). All of these pilots had served in the tripartite evaluation squadron effort and were therefore quite familiar with the XV-6A's (Kestrel's) flight characteristics.

The following pilot's comments on these trials, as well as those occurring with LPD-1 (Landing Port Dock) *U.S.S. Raleigh* (using 64-18266), by Lt. Col. J.K. Campbell, USAF, are a good overview of the results:

"**1.** *Patuxent:* This training phase was most valuable and well managed in preparing pilots for CVA-62 carrier operations. The image of a carrier painted on runway 31 was useful to non-naval pilots in learning carrier terminology and in identifying various takeoff and landing areas. The mirror landing system was easy to use and was of some value from ¼ mile to 1 mile out on final. Taxi operations on the painted deck instilled pilot confidence in the XV-6A maneuverability on board. The value of a landing signal officer (LSO) was controversial.

2. *Carrier Independence (CVA-62): May 11-15*

The following are my impressions pertinent to carrier operation technology:

A. Advantages of V/STOL operations on a carrier:

(1) No elaborate training was required for non-carrier pilots to be able to get on and off on a clear deck or on any portion of clear deck such as bow, waist, or fantail.

(2) The wide variety of airspeeds available to vectored thrust aircraft permit the V/STOL to provide adequate spacing between landing aircraft with slower final approach speeds.

(3) A V/STOL figher can come to a hover and wait for as long as two minutes to get a clear deck to land on.

(4) The scramble time of four XV-6's seemed to be less than for catapult launching of the same number of conventional aircraft.

(5) A marked weight reduction would be possible for conventional V/STOL fighters if arresting gear, catapult structure, beefed-up landing gear, and possibly folding wings (assuming V/STOL aircraft need less wing area) could be deleted.

(6) 'Bolters' (missing the arresting cable) occurred often for conventional aircraft. I have never had to make a 'go-around' or missed approach in an XV-6. Such an advantage should improve the timing for recovery and consequently should ease the command and control problems for large numbers of aircraft.

B. Several heated discussions took place on the carrier regarding marginal XV-6 operations. Some were related to the peculiarities of the airplane, but some were also related to all-jet V/STOL concepts. These were:

(1) Flight while significant rain was falling (or flight through rain showers on the down wind or base leg) was avoided because of the known deficiencies of the XV-6's windscreen rain removal system.

(2) Flight with existing head wind over deck in excess of 30 knots (the XV-6 wind limitation). The XV-6 did accommodate higher wind-over-deck speeds, so as to conform to conventional aircraft takeoff and landing requirements. Certain other designs of jet V/STOL aircraft may not have such a STOL capability, and future U.S. Navy specifications should require good handling qualities in the regime of 0 to 40 knots.

(3) Hovering operations were avoided in the hot gas discharge from the stacks, although some flights were made in the fringe of the exhaust. For future design the characteristics of this exhaust should be defined; the core size and temperature at various distances aft of the island. Perhaps the fuel controller should be designed to cope with sudden changes of aircraft inlet air temperatures to preclude surge, compressor stall, and even gross

U.S. KESTREL SERIAL NUMBER SUMMARY				
Tripartite		**U.S. Tri-Service**		**NASA**
Serial	*Nose*	*A.F. Serial*	*Nose*	
XS688	8	64-18262	2	
XS689	9	64-18263	3	521
XS690	0	64-18264	4	
XS691	1	64-18265	5	
XS692	2	64-18266	6	520
XS694	4	64-18267	7	520

Nose detail of XV-6A (A.F. serial 64-18266) is shown here. Taken in May of 1966, on board the *USS Independence* (CVA-62), this photo shows attitude ball in tip of nose, yaw vane, and XV-6A-peculiar intake lip. Canopy detail is also worth comparing to production AV-8A. *U.S. Navy photo via NATC Patuxent River*

Main gear and rear exhaust nozzle details of XV-6A (A.F. serial 64-18264). Heat shield assembly shown attached to exhaust nozzle fairing and fuselage, is noteworthy. *U.S. Navy photo via NATC Patuxent River*

loss in performance.

(4) Hovering, VTO, VL and taxi operations were limited behind the jet blasts of idling aircraft and behind the catapult blast deflectors when aircraft were running up for takeoff. This is a potential problem for V/STOL aircraft probably not encountered by conventional aircraft and should be considered during "mixed" operations. More powerful steering control and more control power for altitude control may be required to cope with such disturbances.

(5) Hovering high (30 ft. plus) over the edge of the deck was no problem, but hovering lower over the edge may pose a control problem because of the asymmetric effects of reflected jet efflux under the wings and tail. This concern precluded any VTOL directly on or off of the elevators along the edges of the ship.

C. No cross-wind operations, night operations, or IFR operations were conducted; however, it is easy to conjecture that when adequate handling qualities are available for V/STOL aircraft, these aspects should be easier for V/STOL than for conventional aircraft. Such handling qualities should be available when a good limited authority autostabilization system is superimposed onto the present XV-6 manual control system.

3. *Landing Port Dock "Raleigh" (LPD-1): May 17.*

Mixed operations were not necessary as the pilot had the entire deck (measuring 85' x 200') of the LPD 'to himself' during takeoff and landing. It was always possible to approach into the wind and the Captain could easily provide any requested ship heading and speed to accommodate the aircraft. I can easily envision four XV-6's on deck at one time: one on each landing circle and two parked forward by the superstructure. Height control and precise touch-down accuracy was made easier because of the visual reference provided by seeing the superstructure. There was little or no spray problem from the deflection of the jet stream onto the ocean about 80 feet below. I was comfortable taxiing the XV-6 in a 360-degree turn on the deck. No LSO was required, although one was available. No mirror landing system was necessary."

The carrier suitability evaluation trials using the XV-6's totalled at twenty shorebased flights (Patuxent River) and thirty-three aboard the CVA and LPD. No basic problems were discovered and it was noted that piloting techniques developed during the shorebased operations were satisfactory for shipboard operations. The official report concluded that VTOL operations using jet-propelled fixed-wing aircraft were feasible and that jet V/STOL aircraft would greatly increase the operational flexibility of the fleet. Further, the report recommended that additional programs should be implemented to exploit the potential of jet V/STOL airplanes aboard U.S. Navy ships.

Following conclusion of the Navy's carrier trials, the XV-6's were shipped back to Fort Campbell and then the Air Proving Ground Center, Eglin AFB, Florida for the Air Force portion of the Tri-Service tests. These tests were conducted from July 15 to 31, 1966. The aircraft were then distributed to several different user agencies: 64-18262 went to Edwards AFB for Air Force tests along with 64-1864; 64-18263 was taken over by NASA and transferred to Langley AFB, Virginia along with 64-18267 (which had suffered the afore-mentioned hard landing); and 64-18265 had 64-18266 also went to Edwards. It has been reported that NASA paid about $3.4 million for their two airframes.

The two ships turned over to NASA were eventually used in a large number of V/STOL aircraft related test and exploration programs not the least of which were exploration of thrust vectoring in forward flight (better known as VIFF), and evaluations of vectored-thrust-jet V/STOL aircraft during simulated instrument approaches.

Once in the possession of NASA, the two aircraft were given NASA registrations. 64-18263 thus became NASA 521, and 64-18267 became NASA 520. Eventually, 64-18265 and 64-18266 would join these two, but not as flightworthy vehicles — they would be used only for spare parts support.

The VIFF trials officially began with the first official VIFF flight on January 16, 1970. Using NASA 521, the effects of VIFF on the combat maneuverability of the XV-6 were documented and evaluated within a carefully expanded thrust vectoring envelope which ultimately allowed unrestricted use of the rotatable nozzles above 10,000 feet using a fan speed of 90-percent and a maximum Mach number of .9. These

tests were conducted in two general phases: (1) non-turning flight; and (2) turning flight.

The effects of thrust vectoring on the constant-altitude flight maximum speed envelope were defined during envelope expansion tests. Using fixed nozzle angles of 0-degrees, 15-degrees, 30-degrees, and 45-degrees, stabilized constant-altitude performance was explored at a number of power settings between minimum speeds limited by a 12-degree angle of attack and maximum speeds limited by an engine fan speed of 90-percent. Reaction control duct pressures, tailplane required for trim, and static longitudinal stability were documented at each trim point.

The decelerating effects of vectoring gross thrust were documented by rapidly deflecting the nozzles to angles of 60-degrees, 81-degrees, and 95-degrees and increasing the thrust to 90-percent from stabilized entry speeds of 200 to 450 KCAS while attempting to hold pitch attitude constant throughout a 10-second deceleration.

Constant altitude turns and windup turns using nozzle angles of 0-degrees, 15-degrees, and 30-degrees were performed at approximately 16,000 feet at airspeeds from 200 to 450 KCAS to assess the steady-state effects of VIFF on turning performance. The data were taken with a maximum thrust of 90-percent at each stabilized test airspeed.

Shot of XV-6A #6 during thrust pad proof tests at Edwards AFB, California. Taken April 3, 1967. *U.S. Air Force photo 67-1672 via Ted Bear*

Unusual view of XV-6A (A.F. serial 64-18264) mounted on special VTOL rack at Edwards AFB, California. Tests were apparently acoustical in nature as pole mounted devices appear to be acoustical sensors. Date of photo is October 27, 1967. *U.S. Air Force photo 181087 USAF*

Load factor was slowly increased until airspeed and/or altitude could no longer be maintained constant. The data were taken at the maximum load factor achieved at each test condition.

During windup turns, altitude was allowed to vary while load factor was increased at a constant airspeed until wing rock occurred. These turns were more indicative of the maximum lift capability of the airplane combining both aerodynamic and vectored thrust components.

Generally speaking, during the course of these tests, the XV-6's handling qualities in non-vectored flight were considered acceptable for a combat aircraft. Static longitudinal stability was considered weak but positive, allowing the pilot to traverse the combat arena with little or no requirement to retrim stick forces. Pitch response to pilot inputs was immediate and damping of both pitch rate and the longitudinal short period oscillation was adequate. Maneuvering forces were light throughout the speed range of 200 to 450 KCAS. Maneuvering load factor and control force increased progressively with control displacement until the limit angle of attack (15-degrees) or wing rock was reached. The angle-of-attack limitation was based on engine surge considerations due to inlet internal flow separation. Maneuvers were always terminated at wing rock because of the predicted loads imposed on vertical fin structure.

Longitudinal characteristics were altered slightly with the use of thrust vectoring. The immediately obvious qualitative and quantitative difference lay in a rather large and abrupt noseup trim change with initial nozzle deflection. Once the aircraft was retrimmed, static longitudinal stability was apparently neutral becoming slightly negative at the lower speeds. Manuevering forces remained positive at speeds above 200 KCAS; however, the combined effects of high control sensitivity and light static stability made precise offensive tracking of enemy aircraft difficult during both vectored and non-vectored maneuvering at low load factors. It was felt that stability augmentation would be required for effective tracking characteristics.

Lateral directional maneuvering characteristics of the XV-6 were excellent up to the point of wing rock which occurred abruptly. Decreasing the angle of attack effected immediate recovery from the wing rock and no lateral divergence or loss of control was experienced.

The results of the VIFF tests outlined above were that VIFF definitely enhanced the ability of a combat aircraft to decelerate and to turn. The test aircraft had aerodynamic deficiencies which resulted in a relatively low angle-of-attack Dutch roll (wing rock), and was thrust deficient. On the positive side, the XV-6A had acceptable stability and control characteristics for research within the flight envelope investigated. It proved that VIFF provides:

1. A substantial increase in flightpath deceleration capability and rate of application compared to that produced by combined throttle chop and speed brake extension.

2. An appreciable instantaneous increment in normal acceleration with abrupt application of large nozzle deflections at high speed.

3. A significant increase in sustained turn rate capability below approximately .72 Mach.

The NASA terminal area flight tests, again using NASA 521, were flown at

Painted in USAF markings, XV-6A undergoes flight tests over Edwards AFB, California on 10-12-67. Note short loop antenna just ahead of front engine exhaust nozzles. *Air Force photo KE 31379*

NASA 521 was XV-6A used in military-related VIFF trials. Bulge under nose is small gun camera. Note angle of exhaust nozzles during this particular conventional takeoff. *NASA photo L-69-1541*

Top view of NASA 521 shows type's distinctive stubby wing. Flaps and ailerons are clearly delineated. NASA photo L-71-2776

Close-up of NASA 521 nose shows test pitot boom with pitch and yaw vanes, and small gun camera bulge under cockpit. Note round windscreen center panel — Harrier's is flat. *NASA photo L-69-203*

An unusual photo of NASA's two XV-6As. Of special interest are the underwing fuel tanks. *NASA photo L-66-6206 via Derek Monk*

Wallops Station, Virginia. Because of the airplane's inate instabilities in the powered-lift mode, and because there was no safety pilot, simulated instrument approaches were flown by using a "peek-a-boo" instrument flight technique in which the pilot's vision was unobstructed. By using this technique, the pilot's concentration was primarily on his instrument task, but he had the benefit of peripheral visual cues for attitude stabilization and reduced localizer workload. The conversion to powered-lift flight was accomplished both prior to and after glide-slope intercept. During the latter part of the program, decelerating approaches to 65 knots at breakout were completed.

The main part of the program focused on identifying the problems associated with managing powered lift in the terminal area and developing operational techniques utilizing the vectored thrust concept. The research effort concentrated on the conversion to powered-lift flight prior to and after glide-slope acquisition and the use of thrust modulation or nozzle-angle modulation as a means of controlling the glide slope. The stability and control characteristics of the aircraft which hindered the instrument approach task were identified and, in some cases, the required corrections were noted. Problems dealing with the cruise letdown to localizer capture, breakout, flare and landing were examined on a limited basis.

Conclusions of this program were as follows:

1. Although the XV-6 was neutrally stable to unstable about all axes in powered-lift flight, the airplane was easily controlled in visual flight because of a well-tailored control system. The control forces, sensitivities, and harmony were excellent.

2. Because of the lack of stability during powered-lift flight, pitch-attitude stabilization will be required for the instrument landing system approaches. In addition, lateral stability augmentation in terms of roll stabilization with turn coordination and/or heading hold will undoubtedly be required.

3. Conversion from wingborne to powered-lift flight was accomplished more easily after glide-slope acquisition than before glide-slope intercept.

4. Glide-slope tracking by means of thrust modulation was more satisfactory than by means of nozzle angle modulation.

5. Although 11-degree, 65-knot approaches were accomplished, the rate of descent at breakout (6.5 meters per second) was excessive. The most satisfactory was the 7-degree, three-nozzle step decelerating approach, since for this case, the rate of descent was decreased to 4-meters per second at breakout.

6. The programmed decelerating approaches were made without great difficulty and provided a saving in time and fuel.

7. Although recirculation effects near the ground increased pilot workload significantly, they produced no serious control or trim problems.

Tests by NASA and the Air Force using the various surviving XV-6's continued into 1974. However, by this time the aircraft were beginning to outlive their usefulness and newer, more powerful successors were becoming available. Eventually, 64-18262 were placed on display at the Air Force Museum (Wright-Patterson AFB, Ohio); 64-18263 was placed on display in the Smithsonian Institution's National Air & Space Museum; 64-18264 became a target on the armaments test range at Edwards AFB and was used during Northrop A-9 gun tests (rumor has it that '264 is still very much intact — and is quite restorable); 64-18265 is presently at the bottom of the James River having fallen from a helicopter during the course of a transfer flight to the Hampton Virginia Aerospace Park; 64-18266 took '265's place at same; and 64-18267 as

NASA 520, ground looped in 1967, was used for spares and ignominiously scrapped following several years of storage at the government demolition site at the USN Yorktown Naval Weapons Station.

XV-6A (P.1127/Kestrel) PROGRAM COSTS

The P.1127 project was funded approximately equally by each of the three countries, with the United States and United Kingdom shares being about $35.9 million and the Federal Republic of Germany share being $32.3 million. The XV-6A program was under the management of (and funded by) the U.S. Army.

Harrier

Long before the U.S. acquired the six tripartite Kestrels, and some nine months before the tripartite trials had, in fact, ended, Hawker, on February 19, 1965, received a contract from the British Ministry of Supply for six developed versions of the Kestrel designated P.1127 RAF. Hawker had not been sitting still while Kestrel evaluations were taking place within the confines of the tripartite effort. An entirely new airplane had slowly emerged from the drawing boards, this being a Kestrel of much improved performance and greatly increased power.

The six pre-production P.1127 RAF's were allocated registrations XV276 thru XV281. They would be used primarily for research and development work on the new design and would not be scheduled

NASA 520 sits patiently on the ramp at NASA Langley, Virginia. Barely discernible is the fact that the XV-6A's main tires are deflated. Note Ram Air Turbine (RAT) extended on top of fuselage. *NASA photo L-66-6609 via D.E. Monk and Dick Culpepper*

XV-6A was interim configuration between P.1127 and Harrier. NASA 521, shown here, was one of XV-6A's assigned to NASA Langley, Virginia. Note markings indicating angular movement capability of exhaust nozzle. *NASA photo L-74-1369 via D.E. Monk and Dick Culpepper*

for actual operational service with the RAF.

The purpose of the P.1127 RAF was basically to develop a less costly (and therefore, lower performance) aircraft to fulfill Operational Requirement 356, vacated by the now-recently-deceased Hawker P.1154. This had been an extremely advanced, supersonic VTOL aircraft similar in basic design to the P.1127, but substantially more sophisticated and complex. The P.1154 had engendered considerable interest among the various NATO air forces, but had died a tragic death thanks to an overdose of British politics and penny pinching.

By now, Bristol Siddeley had the Pegasus producing nearly 19,000 pounds of thrust. They felt very confident that the engine could guarantee this thrust (and resultant high thrust-to-weight-ratio) in an operational environment. The engine had an all-titanium fan, cooled first and second-stage high-pressure turbines, a revised combustion system with water injection, a revised fuel system, and two-vane nozzles. Thrust was an honest 19,000 pounds and time between overhauls was a reasonable 300 hours. Officially designated Pegasus 6 Mk. 101, it was first bench tested in March of 1965.

The Kestrel and the new P.1127 RAF were two almost totally different aircraft. In fact, the latter demanded nearly 95% new drawings and relied on its predecessor's design for precious little. Among the major changes incorporated were an almost totally new fuselage that allowed the additional internal space required of the Pegasus 6 and its associated fuel; a totally new intake design that allowed greater intake air recovery at all speeds and altitudes and

that incorporated some sixteen blow-in auxiliary doors for increased airflow in hover; a new low authority pitch and roll auto-stabilizer that improved control dramatically in the V/STOL mode; a self-starter for field operations; a new and almost totally redesigned and improved landing gear; a Ferranti inertial navigation system; a Smith's HUD (Heads Up Display); a new and much improved wing planform; the ability to carry external stores (the P.1127 RAF was to have a 12,000 pound operationally equipped weight and a VTOL gross of 16,000 pounds — this allowing a payload of 4,000 pounds for fuel, armament, etc.); four wing and three fuselage hardpoints (two fuselage stations normally carrying 30mm Aden gun pods with 130 rounds per gun); bolt-on extended wingtips for ferry flights; a flight refueling probe and associated systems; and literally hundreds of lesser odds and ends that included everything from cockpit details to color schemes.

It should be noted that a number of items scheduled to equip the new P.1127 RAF had originally been designed for the defunct P.1154. The afore-mentioned Ferranti nav/attack system was among these; it was transferred intact (except for the radar.)

The first pre-production P.1127 RAF, XV276, first flew on August 31, 1966 with test pilot Bedford once again at the controls. By this time, the name Harrier had been chosen for the new airplane (it was originally intended to be the name of the P.1154), this coming from the name of a bird of prey noted for its distinctive low flying hunting technique. In early 1964, the first full-production authorization was granted, this resulting in an order for 60 GR.1's (Ground

attack/Reconnaissance) powered by the 19,000 pound thrust Pegasus 101 and ten similarly powered T.2's (two place tandem-seating trainers). Later, these production orders would be increased to 77 GR.1's and 12 T.2's, and later still, to 93 GR.1's and 15 T.2's. Power would be increased also through the incorporation of the Pegasus 102 which was rated at 20,000 pounds thrust, and the Pegasus 103 rated at 21,500 pounds thrust. Most aircraft would eventually be produced with the last mentioned model, and those not produced with it would be retrofitted.

The first of the true production series Harrier GR.1's, XV738, flew for the first time on December 28, 1967. This airplane incorporated all production-standard features of the operational airplane and was the first to enter operational service with the Royal Air Force.

In the meantime, Kestrel-related work in the U.S. had led to a strong interest in the Hawker Harrier program. Northrop, based on the promise of Harrier developments, had, somewhat surprisingly, received a $330,000 contract from the Pentagon on November 30, 1966 for further XV-6 testing at Edwards AFB.

Marine Corps

Concomitant with this XV-6 activity, three U.S. Marine Corps officers (Brig. Gen. Johnson, Col. T. Miller, and Lt. Col. B. Baker) walked into the Hawker chalet at the 1968 SBAC Airshow and made what amounted to the first official U.S. Marine inquiry into the Harrier program.

The inquiry presented by the Marine threesome had not been a

AV-8A, BuNo 159239 of VMA-231 on board the *U.S.S. Roosevelt* (CV-42) in 1976. Finish is standard camouflage with all markings in black except last two digits of nose number stencilled in white high on the tail. Squadron insignia is black and white. Note that the nose number is in white on the right flap upper surface, and in black on the airbrake inner surface.

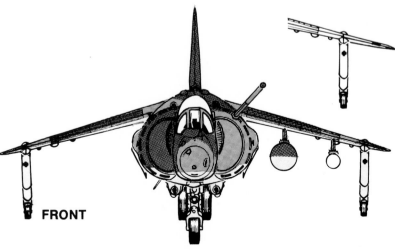

SCALE VIEWS (1/72)

FRONT

VMA-513 emblem
Disc is white and light blue divided down the center and edged in yellow-gold. Owl is white detailed black and yellow-gold. Large cloud is dark blue; stars and moon are yellow-gold; small cloud is white. Banner is black edged in yellow gold. Often only the owl is applied to the unit's aircraft.

VMA-231 emblem
Black disc bordered white; playing card is white with black marking and lettering; banner is white with black lettering.

VMA-542 emblem
Disc is white with yellow-gold tiger detailed in black with green eyes, reddish pink nose, red tongue, and white teeth; lightning flashes are yellow-gold; banner is white with black lettering.

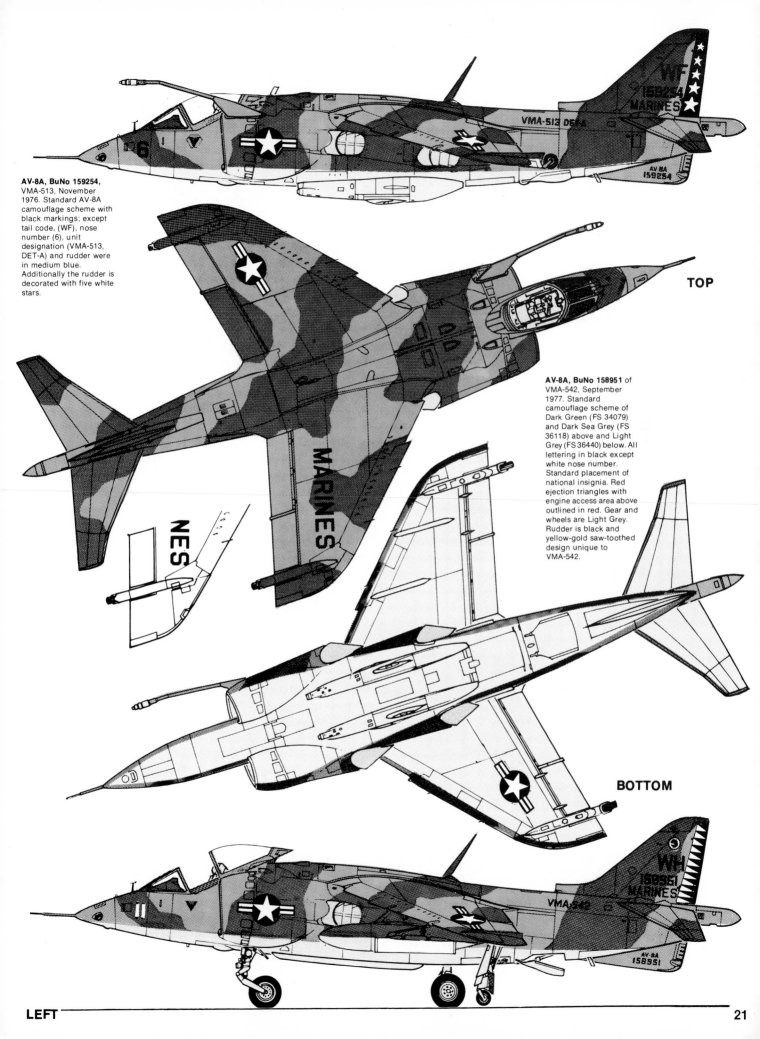

AV-8A, BuNo 159254, VMA-513, November 1976. Standard AV-8A camouflage scheme with black markings; except tail code, (WF), nose number (6), unit designation (VMA-513, DET-A) and rudder were in medium blue. Additionally the rudder is decorated with five white stars.

TOP

AV-8A, BuNo 158951 of VMA-542, September 1977. Standard camouflage scheme of Dark Green (FS 34079) and Dark Sea Grey (FS 36118) above and Light Grey (FS 36440) below. All lettering in black except white nose number. Standard placement of national insignia. Red ejection triangles with engine access area above outlined in red. Gear and wheels are Light Grey. Rudder is black and yellow-gold saw-toothed design unique to VMA-542.

BOTTOM

LEFT

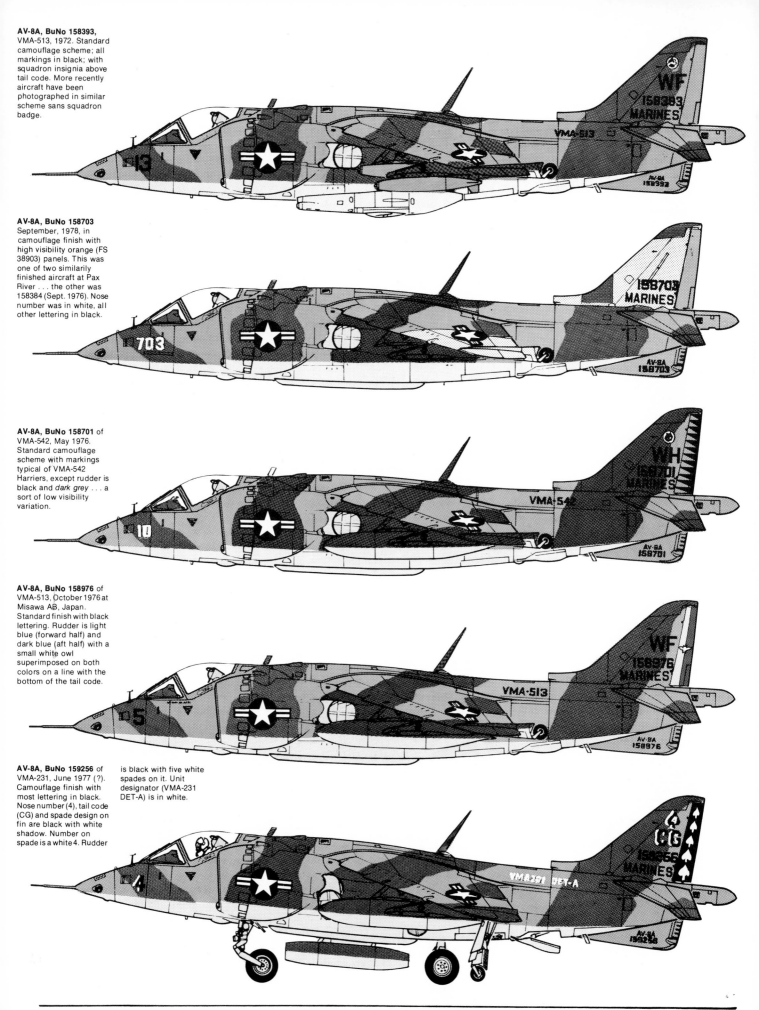

AV-8A, BuNo 158393,
VMA-513, 1972. Standard camouflage scheme; all markings in black; with squadron insignia above tail code. More recently aircraft have been photographed in similar scheme sans squadron badge.

AV-8A, BuNo 158703
September, 1978, in camouflage finish with high visibility orange (FS 38903) panels. This was one of two similarly finished aircraft at Pax River . . . the other was 158384 (Sept. 1976). Nose number was in white, all other lettering in black.

AV-8A, BuNo 158701 of VMA-542, May 1976. Standard camouflage scheme with markings typical of VMA-542 Harriers, except rudder is black and *dark grey* . . . a sort of low visibility variation.

AV-8A, BuNo 158976 of VMA-513, October 1976 at Misawa AB, Japan. Standard finish with black lettering. Rudder is light blue (forward half) and dark blue (aft half) with a small white owl superimposed on both colors on a line with the bottom of the tail code.

AV-8A, BuNo 159256 of VMA-231, June 1977 (?). Camouflage finish with most lettering in black. Nose number (4), tail code (CG) and spade design on fin are black with white shadow. Number on spade is a white 4. Rudder is black with five white spades on it. Unit designator (VMA-231 DET-A) is in white.

spur-of-the-moment event. The Marine Corps had maintained a strong commitment to V/STOL aircraft for more than 20 years and it was obvious that the Harrier was where the future lay. This commitment had been formally stated on July 23, 1957, when the Commandaent of the Marine Corps, General Randolph McC. Pate, delivered a letter to the Chief of Naval Operations that read in part: "Vertical takeoff and landing characteristics are an ultimate requirement of all Marine aircraft in support of amphibious operations in the future . . . Obtaining a STOL/VTOL capability is vital to Marine aviation."

In 1963, when technology had progressed to the point where it appeared possible that V/STOL aircraft could be competitive with Conventional Takeoff and Landing (CTOL) aircraft, the Marine Mid-Range Objective Plan stated: "V/STOL capability will be included in the requirement for any aircraft if it provides a worthwhile improvement in operational effectiveness without unacceptably degrading flight performance or unduly increasing overall support and maintenance."

The advantages of V/STOL were again formally stated in 1965, in "Marine Corps-85, a Long Range Study." The recommendations of this study led to the statement of a requirement for the Harrier in December of 1968.

Underscoring this Marine interest, Marine General G. McCutcheon, well-aware of the U.S. XV-6A flight test program (and very impressed with what he had seen) had, in 1968, birthed a scheme wherein it was determined that the Marine Corps would be an all V/STOL force by the end of the following decade. It had been three of McCutcheon's disciples who had visited the Hawker chalet in 1968.

In-mid 1968, the Air Weapons Requirements Branch under McCutcheon briefed him on the improvements that had been incorporated in the Kestrel to make it into the Harrier. At that point it was decided that it was time to investigate Harrier performance first hand. The Commandant, General L. Chapman, and McCutcheon, agreed to send Col. Tom Miller and Lt. Col. Bud Baker (both test pilots of extensive experience) to England to see if they might be permitted to fly the Harrier.

After detailed negotiations with the British Embassy, and the help of the Defense Supply Attache, Capt. John Glendinning, Royal Navy, the British agreed to allow Miller and Baker to fly the Harrier following the Farnborough Airshow in September 1968. They became the first non-British pilots to do so.

After reporting the results of their flights to Generals Chapman and McCutcheon, the decision was made for the Marine Corps to attempt to get DoD and Congressional approval to procure some Harriers in order to prove a concept of operations.

Following this decision, McCutcheon and Miller convinced Vice Admiral T. Connally, then Deputy Chief of Naval Operations (Aviation) to send three Navy test pilots and one Navy fleet pilot to England to confirm Miller's and Baker's findings and opinions. These pilots soon returned, even more enthusiastic about the Harrier than Miller and Baker. Shortly after this effort, the U.S. Air Force, for

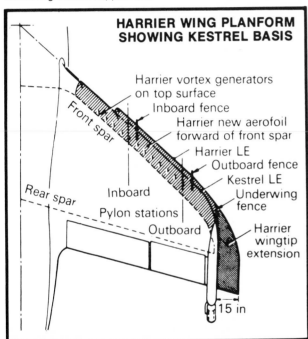

HARRIER WING PLANFORM SHOWING KESTREL BASIS

Harrier vortex generators on top surface
Inboard fence
Harrier new aerofoil forward of front spar
Harrier LE
Outboard fence
Kestrel LE
Underwing fence
Harrier wingtip extension

Front spar
Rear spar
Inboard
Pylon stations
Outboard
15 in

Close-up of second USMC Harrier under construction at Hawker Siddeley. Engine bay, as can be seen, is quite large. *Hawker Siddeley photo 701553*

Unusual photo showing the third and fourth AV-8A's for Marine Corps service. Photo taken inside Hawker Siddeley plant approximately three-quarters of the way down the Harrier production line. *Hawker Siddeley photo 701540*

fear of being left behind, also sent two pilots to England to fly the Harrier. It was during this latter visit that the first fatality of the program occurred when one of the visiting USAF pilots, Maj. Charles Rosberg, was killed.

By December of 1968, the Commandant of the Marine Corps had become a very strong supporter of the Harrier and its capabilities, and through the help of many persons in DoD and industry, not to mention the strong support given by the President's Scientific Advisory Committee on Tactical Aircraft, was able to eventually get Presidential and Congressional approval for procurement of 12 Harriers for evaluation and service test purposes. Unfortunately, the Marines were forced to give up $58-million for the procurement of 17 new F-4B's in order to pay for the Harriers.

Once the Marine Corps was assured that it would get 12 Harriers, Maj. Bud Iles, a test pilot, and Capt. "Speedy" Gonzales, a maintenance officer, were sent to England to serve in the RAF squadrons which were already operational.

It is interesting to note that Air Force and Navy interest in the Harrier had been anything but non-existant. In fact, quite the opposite was the case, though public expression of this enthusiastic interest was severely restrained. Perhaps the most obvious acknowledgement of the Harrier's attractiveness was the fact that both the Air Force and Navy had sent evaluation pilots to England to examine and fly early production examples.

On April 1, 1969, the Harrier began operational service with the Royal Air Force. Within weeks of this activity, a U.S. liaison team and Harrier Project Office was set up at Mintech.

Marine Corps Harrier funding was finally approved by Congress in mid-1969. The initial order was for 12 single-seat Hawker Mk.50 series aircraft,

officially given the U.S. designation AV-8A (AV standing for Attack, Vertical Takeoff and Landing). These were basically British RAF GR. 1 models with modifications to meet Marine Corps specifications. Among the latter were a different IFF (Identification, Friend or Foe) system, provision for the carrying of Sidewinder air-to-air-missiles, an altimeter and a HUD that read in inches of mercury instead of milibars, and provisions for an assortment of U.S-manufactured and designed air-to-ground weapons.

By this time, McDonnell Douglas had awakened to the Harrier's unique capabilities and had applied for and received permission to take over the U.S. production rights which Northrop had allowed to lapse. It was hoped by McDonnell Douglas that the additional 102 aircraft requested by the Marines, over and above the original order for 12, could be produced indigenously in the U.S. If such a plan were to be approved, it stated that the first McDonnell Douglas built aircraft could be delivered in 1971, assuming that many primary components could be acquired outright from Hawker. By 1975, it was expected that the airplane would be totally U.S. made.

Problems with McDonnell Douglas' plans eventually led to a buy of a further 100-percent British-built aircraft in lots of 18, 30, and 30. By 1973, 90 AV-8A Harriers had been bought by the Marine Corps. In 1974, an additional buy of 24 aircraft was approved, but this figure (which would have brought the total buy to 114 including the original 12 aircraft) was cut by 4 before final approval. The final buy thus became twenty aircraft consisting of 12 AV-8A's and 8 two-place TAV-8A's (which was the cause behind

VMA-513 AV-8A (BuNo. 158384) in flight during operations from Patuxent River, Maryland. Note rather large inflight refueling probe mounted above port intake. *U.S. Navy photo KN-19420*

the four airplane cutback — due to their slightly higher unit cost). The last buy amounted to a total expense of $58.2-million (which included the costs of ground support equipment and spares) for the AV-8A's and $53.6 million for the TAV-8A's. The Marine Corps thus ended their AV-8 acquisition program at this point with a total of 110 aircraft.

Following delivery of the first AV-8A on November 20, 1970, Board of Inspection and Survey (BIS) trials took place at Patuxent River, Maryland. Because the AV-8A was an off-the-shelf operational aircraft, it did not require the normal U.S. research and development program normally associated with new aircraft. The first four AV-8A's were utilized for the trials which took place at the Naval

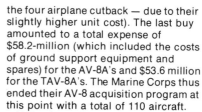

Awaiting takeoff instruction, the British exchange pilot of this gloss-paint Marine AV-8A sits patiently as the deck is cleared. Photo taken aboard the *USS Guadalcanal* (LPH-7) in 1971 during exercises in the Atlantic Ocean. *U.S. Navy photo K-89307 by Wade Davis*

Carrier suitability tests of the Marines first Harrier (BuNo. 158384) aboard the *U.S.S. Coronado* (LPD-11). These tests were conducted during April, 1971, at Norfolk, Virginia. *U.S. Marine Corps photo by D.C. Motley*

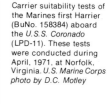

The U.S. Marine Corps first AV-8A (BuNo. 158384) as it appeared at Pax River in March 1971, just two months after delivery. Markings of VMA-513 have been applied over a still very high-gloss factory finish. *U.S. Marine Corps photo A701597 by R.A. Rees*

Air Test Center. BIS trials took some four months to complete and consisted primarily of some 200 sorties exploring various aspects of the airplane's declared operational role. No other test programs were required.

The BIS trials revealed that the AV-8A could be flown from short, relatively unprepared locations and could be depended upon to accurately deliver a wide variety of tactical ordnance. Excellent reliability and the relatively small amount of servicing required between flights made the airplane well adapted to quick turnarounds and high sortie rates.

After the BIS trials, a joint CNO/CMC directive of August 27, 1970, formally established Project Battle Cry to operationally appraise the AV-8A's performance and the V/STOL concept of operations. Project Battle Cry was established initially for the tactical deployment of the AV-8A and for the preparation of the AV-8A Tactical Manual. The scope of Battle Cry was expanded to include an evaluation of V/STOL as it applies to long range developments of aircraft for the Navy and Marine Corps. Project Battle Cry encompassed weapon delivery, defensive fighter tactics, shipboard compatibility, forward basing, sortie rate validation and training requirements,

plus related tests of communications, command and control and logistic support of the V/STOL concept of operations.

MARINE AV-8's TODAY

The AV-8A's and TAV-8A's now in Marine Corps service currently equip four squadrons including three tactical squadrons of 15 aircraft and 22 pilots each, and a training squadron. These consist of Marine Attack Squadron 513 (VMA-513) based at the Marine Corps Air Station, Yuma, Arizona; Marine Attack Squadron 542 (VMA-542) based at the Marine Corps Air Station, Cherry Point, North Carolina; Marine Attack Squadron 231 (VMA-231) based at the Marine Corps Air Station, Cherry Point, North Carolina; and Marine Attack Training Squadron 203 (VMAT-203) based at the Marine Corps Air Station, Cherry Point, North Carolina.

Marine tactical planners have mated the Harrier's effectiveness in the close air support role with a unique scheme of maneuver for amphibious assault which is based on flexibility in basing the airplane virtually anywhere in range of combat troops.

This flexibility is a key advantage of the V/STOL AV-8 and provides for operations from multiple type sea bases, early movement ashore, operations from

austere sites ashore, rapid response for close air support, rapid turn-around for continued sorties, and improved survivability realized from dispersion of the aircraft. These advantages allow the Marine Corps to exploit the capabilities of their tactical attack aircraft much earlier in the amphibious scenario than ever before.

The AV-8 can be positioned very close to ground units and to enemy targets which allows it to be rapidly integrated into the fire support and maneuver plans for Marine ground units. Simplified command and control procedures and pre-briefing of pilots who sit and wait on-call in their aircraft, put the AV-8 just minutes away from answering a call for help in combat.

The operational concept developed by the Marine Corps for the AV-8 exploits the unique capabilities of the aircraft to provide highly responsive close air support during all phases of an amphibious operation.

The AV-8 is based on ships of an Amphibious Task Force while en route to the objective area. Some ships are capable of providing the AV-8 with full support. These ships are called sea bases (main bases afloat) and are either LPH (Landing Platform, Helicopter) or LHA (Landing Helicopter Assault) carriers. When dispersal at sea on

V/STOL SEA BASES

SHIP CLASS	CLASS NAME	SHIP TYPE	TONNAGE	SHIPS IN CLASS	NOMINAL FLIGHT DECK (FT)	NOTES
LPH	Iwo Jima	Amphibious Assault	18,300	7	84 x 592	primary base
LHA	Tarawa	Amphibious Assault	39,300	5	107 x 820	primary base
CV	various	Attack Carriers	various	16	various	secondary base
				TOTAL 28		

VTOL SEA PLATFORMS

With Flight Deck Sizes of At Least 60 x 60 Ft and Loadings of 20,000 Lb

SHIP CLASS	CLASS NAME	SHIP TYPE	TONNAGE	SHIPS IN. CLASS	NOMINAL FLIGHT DECK (FT)
LPD-1	Raleigh	Amphibious Transport Dock	14,600	2	79 x 198
LPD-4	Auston	Amphibious Transport Dock	16,900	12	80 x 234
LCC-19	Blue Ridge	Amphibious Command	17,100	2	74 x 98
LKA-112	Tulare	Amphibious Cargo Ship	16,800	1	62 x 91
LKA-113	Charleston	Amphibious Cargo Ship	20,700	5	76 x 74
LSD-36	Anchorage	Dock Landing Ship	13,700	5	80 x 85
AE-21	Suribachi	Ammunition Ship	17,400	2	69 x 106
AE-23	Nitro	Ammunition Ship	17,500	3	62 x 95
AE-26	Kilauea	Ammunition Ship	19,900	10	72 x 96
AF-58	Rigel	Stores Ship	15,500	1	63 x 81
AFS-1	Mars	Combat Stores Ship	16,300	7	73 x 92
AGF-3	La Salle	Command Ship	13,900	1	75 x 109
AOE-1	Sacramento	Fast Combat Support	52,500	4	84 x 97
AOR-1	Wichita	Replenishment Oiler	38,100	7	85 x 102
				62	

OTHER AIR CAPABLE SHIPS

Potential VTOL Sea Platforms

SHIP CLASS	CLASS NAME	SHIP TYPE	TONNAGE	SHIPS IN. CLASS	NOMINAL FLIGHT DECK (FT)
DD-963	Spruance	Destroyer	7,600	Up to 30	70 x 40
DDG-47	—	Guided Missile Destroyer	9,500	Up to 16	70 x 42
LSD-28	Thomaston	Dock Landing Ship	11,525	8	71 x 53
LST-1179	Newport	Tank Landing Ship	8,400	20	69 x 65
—	—	Container Ships (RMSDS)	27,000	100*	200 x 65

*Approximately 200 if NATO Merchant Ships are counted

There are also about 100 container ships that can be added to the list of potential VTOL platforms. These container ships belong to the merchant marine and are part of the USN's Reserve Merchant Ship Defense System (RMSDS).

smaller ships is required, the AV-8's can be based on sea platforms which are smaller ships capable of providing more limited support to the aircraft.

AV-8 operations in support of landing forces occur in three distinct phases:

Phase I — Operations from Sea Bases
Phase II — Emplacement of the V/STOL Facility
Phase III — Establishment of a Main Base.

During Phase I, AV-8's operate from sea bases. V/STOL flexibility enhances sea-based operations since the AV-8 can be launched and recovered at any time with little regard to ship course or speed. Catapults or arresting gear are not required.

The resulting operational flexibility provides a major improvement in the timeliness and effectiveness of CAS during the assault phase of amphibious operations. It is likely that clear, unprepared surfaces in the beachhead area will soon be captured which can be used for limited AV-8 operations. These areas, which may be as small as 72 feet in diameter, are called forward sites. AV-8's are normally positioned in these forward sites as soon as they are taken to provide the ground commander with ultra-timely response to requests for air support, maximum use of the element of surprise and economic utilization of personnel and material assets since the aircraft are committed only when needed and do not "litter" the air.

When the AV-8 has been used for close air support from a forward site, it returns to a sea base for rearming and refueling.

As ground operations expand in scope and move inland, responsive air support from sea bases becomes increasingly difficult. To insure that close air support is completely responsive throughout the combat operation, AV-8's are moved ashore as soon as it becomes feasible to do so.

In Phase II, AV-8's operate from a facility or a small airfield which has the capability of providing basic support for shore-based operations. Refueling, rearming and minor maintenance can be performed at these facilities ashore. AV-8 operations can be sustained for highly-responsive close air support within the beachhead area using these land facilities.

In low intensity or short duration operations, the option exists to continue

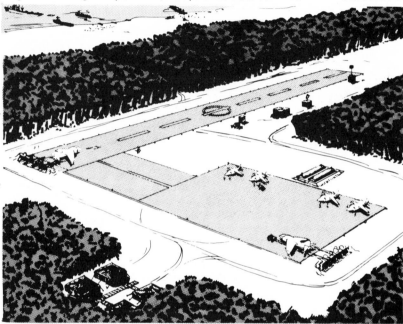

V/STOL FACILITY

Ground crewman of VMA-542, 2nd MAW, directs his pilot from a "hide" at Landing Zone

Lark, Camp Lejeune, North Carolina. *U.S. Marine Corps photo A 343460 by D.A. Delgado*

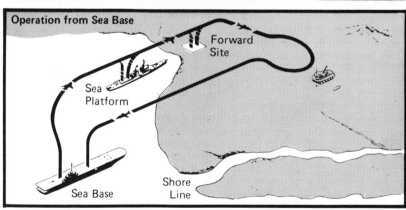

Operation from Sea Base

Forward Site

Sea Platform

Sea Base

Shore Line

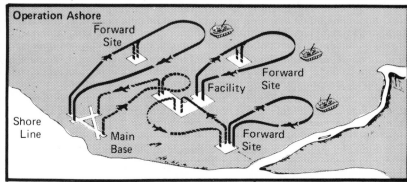

Operation Ashore

Forward Site

Forward Site

Facility

Shore Line

Main Base

Forward Site

Camouflage netting and rudimentary matting provide a

home-away-from-home for this AV-8A of VMA-542. *U.S. Marine Corps photo*

BASING FLEXIBILITY

AV-8 operation from such facilities providing maximum support without having to deal with massive amounts of construction and equipment installation. If the amphibious operation is a lengthy one or involves large land forces, maximum shore-based close air support operations will be required and Phase III, the establishment of a Main Base ashore, will be initiated.

The Main Base will normally be a facility improved by the addition of equipment necessary for complete support of AV-8 operations. Once the Main Base is established, the AV-8's will be independent of the sea bases and capable of operations from facilities and forward sites supported from the main base. It is noteworthy that the main base, with complete AV-8 support, was considerably smaller than the most austere base which will support a conventional, fixed-wing aircraft.

AV-8 OPERATIONAL HIGHLIGHTS

More than 113,000 AV-8A flight hours have been accumulated through July of 1980 by the Marine Corps and essentially all these flight hours are operational. The AV-8A has been employed in many major exercises involving other aircraft types and both land and amphibious forces. In addition, AV-8A's have accumulated extensive experience aboard ships, including all major U.S. Navy air capable ship types. Some of the highlights of the AV-8A operational experience are summarized below:

HIGHLIGHT	ACCOMPLISHMENT
Quick Responsiveness	11.4 minute average from request to bombs on target from forward basing during Versatile Warrior
High Sortie Rate	6.3 average and 10.2 maximum sorties per day per AV-8A during 10 day Versatile Warrior
Forward Site Buildup	Flight operations seven hours after equipment landed by helicopter
Operation from Forward Site	92 Sorties flown from VTOL pads during Versatile Warrior
Operation from Facility	Operated from Bluebird, North Carolina and 29 Palms, California
Operation from Main Base	Operated from Bogue Field, North Carolina
Operation from Sea Base	Operated from LPH, LHA, and CV, including integrated operations with helicopters
Independent Detachment	Maintenance facilities contained in vans taken aboard and operated from LPH-9
Command and Control	CAS operations within existing command and control systems
High Availability	88% of flights (376) during Versatile Warrior returned in up status
VTOL Mission	3000 lb of ordnance carried and expended on a mission of 50 nm radius
Thrust Vector Control for ACM	The Marine Corps has developed tactical uses of inflight thrust vectoring to enhance survivability in ACM engagements
Intercept Capability	Successful visual intercepts of Russian "Shadow" aircraft during sea operations
Safety Record	32 aircraft lost during first 113,000 flight hours — one of the best records of U.S. tactical jet aircraft.
CV Deployment	AV-8A was completely integrated into normal CV air group operations
Suez Canal Transit	AV-8A is only operational jet fixed-wing aircraft to transit the Suez Canal aboard ship
Accepted for Service Use	On 19 September 1974, the Secretary of the Navy published a letter officially accepting the AV-8A for service use
Unprepared Field Operations	Extensive experience with grass fields, dirt strips, and other unprepared sites
NATO Interoperability	Six AV-8As operated from NATO bases during Northern Wedding/Bold Guard

The AV-8A has proven in over eight years of operational Marine Corps (and RAF) uses that V/STOL aircraft meet the close air support requirements of the Marine Corps and that the V/STOL concept of operations is viable.

An overhead view of the amphibious transport dock USS Raleigh (LPD-1) with two Marine AV-8A's on the rear helicopter platform. U.S. Navy photo 1157056

This shot, taken during project "Battle Cry" in 1973 shows an AV-8A hovering over the USS Raleigh (LPD-1). U.S. Navy photo 1157054 by Duncan Groner III

The U.S.S. Tarawa (LHA-1) is representative of the LHA class of Amphibious Assault ships intended among other things, as a primary base for AV-8s. U.S. Navy photo 1166267

This head-on aerial bow view of U.S.S. Belleau Wood (LHA-3) provides a good comparison with the U.S.S. Guadalcanal. U.S. Navy photo 1173118

KESTREL/HARRIER EXPERIENCE AT SEA . . . U.S. NAVY/U.S. MARINE CORPS

	Ship		Tonnage	Date of First Embarkation	Flight Deck	Deck Height Above Sea
CVA	USS Independence *		78,000	May 1966	1047 x 252 ft	65 ft
	USS F. D. Roosevelt		64,000	June 1976	979 x 238 ft	60 ft
LPH	USS Guam		18,300	Jan 1972	590 x 105 ft	54 ft
	USS Iwo Jima		18,300	Oct 1975	592 x 104 ft	54 ft
	USS Tripoli		18,300	Aug 1974	592 x 104 ft	54 ft
	USS Inchon		18,300	Jan 1975	582 x 105 ft	54 ft
	USS Guadalcanal		18,300	Mar 1971	590 x 105 ft	54 ft
	USS New Orleans		18,300	Dec 1975	592 x 104 ft	54 ft
LPD	USS LaSalle		13,900	May 1969	200 x 84 ft	35 ft
	USS Raleigh *		13,900	May 1966	200 x 84 ft	35 ft
	USS Juneau		16,900	Feb 1976	200 x 84 ft	35 ft
	USS Coronado		16,800	Mar 1971	200 x 84 ft	35 ft
	USS Trenton		16,800	Feb 1977	195 x 76 ft	35 ft
	USS Ponce		16,800	Feb 1975	204 x 76 ft	35 ft

*XV-6A TRI-SERVICE TESTS

UNIQUE Capabilities

Besides its obvious vertical takeoff and landing attributes, the AV-8 also benefits from two relatively recently discovered performance capabilities that are unmatched by any other operational airplane in the world.

As already mentioned in the Kestrel section, in 1971, NASA established a flight test program to determine the effect of Thrust Vectoring In Forward Flight (VIFF) on air combat capability of AV-8 type aircraft. When it was confirmed that VIFF enhanced the maneuverability of the aircraft as had been predicted, the test program was expanded as a joint NASA/RAE (Royal Aeronautical Establishment) program to be conducted in two phases.

The first phase began in October of 1972, with several pilots using the differential maneuvering simulator at NASA's Langley Research Center in a large number of combat situations. A Harrier, using VIFF was pitted against a Harrier with nozzles fixed aft. The Harrier using VIFF almost always "won" the combat even when starting in a

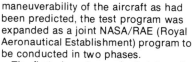

An AV-8A of VMA-513 taxies around the flight deck of the *U.S.S. Juneau* (LPD-10) following the first ever landing of a Harrier aboard an LPD in the Pacific. *U.S. Marine Corps photo A801685*

Six AV-8A's occupy deck space aboard the *USS Guam* (LPH-9) during sea control tests in the Atlantic Ocean. *Hawker Siddeley photo 743527*

Aerial view of the *U.S.S. Tripoli* (LPH-10), a typical LPH, underway. This is one of two classes of Amphibious Assault ships specified as a primary base of Harriers. *U.S. Navy photo 1116550*

Aerial view of the *U.S.S. Guadalcanal* (LPH-7) provides a good idea of the flight deck arrangement of an LPH. *U.S. Navy photo 1169915 by J. Mancias, Jr.*

defensive position. This was followed by flight trials pitting a Harrier against F-4's, Hawker Hunters, Harriers with nozzles fixed aft, and even several captured Soviet aircraft of an unknown type. The success of the Harrier in these engagements was found to be due to the additional lift, deceleration, and nose-up pitch generated by VIFF.

Phase II trials were conducted in Britain in October and November of 1975 and provided the largest data base ever generated by flight trials in which VIFF was used. The trials were divided into medium and low-altitude engagements with the following purposes:

1. Study the effectiveness of VIFF in medium altitude air combat against a low energy threat (simulated by a Hawker Hunter Mk.6) and against a high energy threat (simulated by a BAC Lightning Mk.3).

2. Study the effects of constraining combat to a low altitude band against the same two aircraft. It was intended that this band extend from an altitude of 2,000 feet to 6,000 feet, but these altitudes varied somewhat depending on weather conditions.

3. Compare the engagement results when the Harrier used VIFF with the results when it did not use VIFF.

A developed batch Harrier was modified to expand the VIFF operating envelope and was flown against a Lightning and a Hunter in one-on-one close-in air combat. Four RAF (two adversary and two Harrier) pilots and one USMC pilot flew 103 low and medium altitude engagements against the Lightning followed by three to four engagements against the Hunter. Basic data were recorded onboard the Harrier and Hunter and at radar tracking sites for all three aircraft. Each radar site tracked one aircraft during these engagements.

For an aircraft such as the Harrier that is not designed primarily as an air superiority fighter, survivability is its primary concern in air combat. The results of the Phase II VIFF trials showed that the Harrier had a very high survivability against both threat aircraft in both the medium and low altitude engagements. This was apparent from the paucity of weapon opportunities available to the Hunter and Lightning. As in previous trials and simulations, the Harrier's use of VIFF significantly improved its performance when compared to engagements in which it was not used.

The following is quoted, with permission, from the Number Six issue of ROLLS ROYCE MAGAZINE:

In the following article, Lt. Col. Harry Blot, USMC, provides a personal account of tests undertaken to explore the benefits of using vectored thrust in forward flight (VIFF). He tells how the experience proved this feature to give the Harrier V/STOL light attack aircraft a dramatic increase in air combat vectoring ability makes it very difficult for even advanced supersonic fighters to intercept and destroy the subsonic Harrier.

The first look at thrust vectoring took place during the tests at NATC. Since the RAF had been using VIFF for several years and test sorties were at a premium. I decided just to look at the 500 knot, full reverse thrust point, without any

AV-8As of VMA-513 secured aboard the *U.S.S. Guam* (LPH-9) during interim sea control ship tests. *U.S. Navy photo 1151411 by C.V. Sneed*

Ready for launch, an AV-8A (BuNo. 158387) prepares to depart the deck of the *USS Guam* (LPH-9) during interim sea control ship tests in the Atlantic Ocean. *U.S. Navy photo 1151416 by C.V. Sneed*

Joining several other Harriers aboard the *U.S.S. Guam* (LPH-9) is this AV-8A (BuNo158962) of VMA-513. *U.S. Marine Corps photo A452565 by L.D. Todd*

intermediate checks.

Before I describe the results of this end-point test, I must explain something about my personal strap-in procedure. Due to a strong belief that it is of vital importance to be able to keep track of other airplanes, especially when they are behind you, I only loosely attach myself to the seat, thus allowing maximum freedom of movement and visibility. The penalty of course is that you are free to bounce around the cockpit if the airplane makes any violent maneuvers.

Now back to the 500 knot point. I tried to picture myself in a position where an imagined attacker was closing in for the kill and I had to slow down as fast as possible to cause an overshoot. To quantify the maneuver, I was going to time my deceleration from 500 to 300 knots.

With pencil in hand I slammed the nozzle lever into the braking stop (reverse thrust) position. The airplane started decelerating at an alarming rate, the magnitude of which I could not

VMA-513 AV-8A eases off deck of *USS Guam* (LPH-9) during 1975 exercises in Mediterranean Sea. *U.S. Navy photo 1165991 by L.M. Mackay*

Crewmen on board the *USS Guam* (LPH-9) prepare an AV-8A for flight during 1972 interim sea control ship testing in the Atlantic Ocean. Note pylon-mounted multiple ejector racks and intake plugs for FOD protection. *U.S. Navy photo K-95053*

Aircraft from VMA-513 prepare for take-off from the flight deck of the *U.S.S. Guam* (LPH-9) while on a Mediterranean cruise in late 1975. *U.S. Marine Corps photo A452581 by L.D. Todd*

Conventional STOL takeoff by AV-8A during Atlantic Ocean operations aboard *USS Guam* (LPH-9). Takeoff was not catapult assisted. What appears to be steam from catapult is actually condensation created by engine exhaust contacting wet surface of carrier deck. *U.S. Navy photo*

31

determine because my nose was pressed up against the gunsight. A terrible way to be, even in an imagined conflict. My movements were even further constrained by the fact that the violence of the maneuver had dislodged me from the seat and I was now straddling the stick with my right hand extended backwards between my legs trying to hold on for dear life. Obviously positive 'g's' were out of the question! As the airplane slowed and the forces reduced, I was able to push myself back into the seat and regain control.

Two lessons were learned. I was going to have to compromise my strap-in procedures: and the potential of VIFF was awesome. If somehow the tremendous forces associated with thrust vectoring could be harnessed in a more meaningful fashion, then stand by world, a new dog fighter was coming your way!

A POSITIVE SIDE EFFECT

Due to the limited duration of the NATC trials, the next step took place at Beaufort, South Carolina, home of the Marine's first Harrier squadron, VMA-513. By this time, we had realized that the airplane had some unusual characteristics when the nozzles were deflected. For one thing the nose pitched up about 30 degrees, a fact the aerodynamicists were very unhappy with. Secondly, the reaction controls were automatically activated by the nozzles and could be used to control the airplane below normal stall speed. A new portion of the envelope was starting to open up — low speed.

How to develop tactics to take advantage of these characteristics now became the problem. A contractor was hired to evaluate the effects of VIFF using a computer simulation. The results indicated that the turning capability of the airplane could be enhanced, but the loss of energy associated with VIFF would offset any gains. Not very encouraging.

The computer program was then inserted into the manned ACM simulator at the McDonnell Douglas (MCAIR) plant in St. Louis. This simulator allowed a pilot in one cockpit to fly against another pilot in a different cockpit with the computer acting as the go-between. The results were portrayed on a wrap around screen accompanied by sound effects so that a high degree of realism was attained.

The effort indicated that the effects of VIFF were far more impressive than those predicted by the pure computer. Several good defensive maneuvers were identified, along with a first look at the use of full engine thrust (combat plug) in ACM.

The only anomalies encountered appeared when the nozzles were deflected at lowish speeds. First, the model in the computer did not turn as well as the actual airplane when light stick forces and small nozzle angles were used. When MCAIR changed the simulator to match the turn rates my memory recognized as being correct, I was told that it was aerodynamically impossible for the Harrier to achieve such rates.

The second and most disturbing of the anomalies occurred when violent maneuvering was done while using thrust vectoring at low speeds. My first indication that all was not well was during a dogfight when the nose of the airplane started a slow, undamped oscillation up and down when I used a large amount of VIFF and back stick. As the airspeed decayed, the amplitude of the pitch increased until, at 180 knots, the airplane started to tumble nose over tail. Regardless of what I did, the simulated plane continued to flip until it hit the ground.

Although this maneuver completely befuddled my opponent, I did not categorize it as an enhancing characteristic of VIFF. The situation was repeated several times with the same results. I was becoming quite used to seeing alternating views of houses, sky, fields, clouds, etc.

The seriousness of this episode was that it took place in a portion of the flight envelope that had not been thoroughly explored, at least by the U.S., thus the simulator reaction had to be accepted as the best indication of what was to come. Undaunted, I put on my white scarf, changed my shorts, and returned to Beaufort to verify the results using an actual Harrier.

Fortunately, the tumbling maneuver turned out to be a fault of the simulation rather than the airplane. However, it cost several excess sorties to determine this, since I was unwilling just to rush out and test the worst case point, but rather chose to approach it in an incremental manner.

The turn rate discrepancy was verified by actual flight test. Under certain circumstances, the Harrier would turn faster than theoretically possible. It wasn't until the AV-8B wind tunnel tests were conducted that this was fully understood. It seems that when a small nozzle deflection angle is used and the airplane is in a buffet-free condition, a pumping action is set up that smooths the flow of air across the wing. Essentially, a form of boundary layer control (blown wing) is invoked; a positive side effect of VIFF that no one had predicted. This phenomenon is a little tricky to learn to use, but once mastered enables the pilot to perform tasks previously considered impossible.

NEUTRALIZING AN ENEMY

Now the time came to tie the package together and hopefully produce something operationally useful. Preliminary results indicated that our

A pair of VMA-513 Harriers depart Offutt AFB following a conventional takeoff. Note that the far aircraft (158954) carries electro-luminescent formation light strips on the nose and tail while the near aircraft (158968) doesn't. This is a fairly recent retrofit to the Harrier fleet. *George Cockle photo*

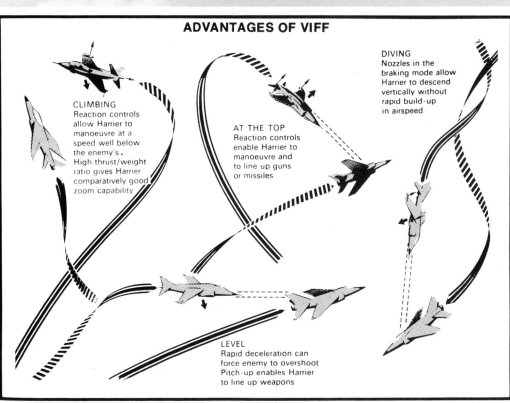

ADVANTAGES OF VIFF

CLIMBING
Reaction controls allow Harrier to manoeuvre at a speed well below the enemy's. High thrust/weight ratio gives Harrier comparatively good zoom capability

AT THE TOP
Reaction controls enable Harrier to manoeuvre and to line up guns or missiles

DIVING
Nozzles in the braking mode allow Harrier to descend vertically without rapid build-up in airspeed

LEVEL
Rapid deceleration can force enemy to overshoot Pitch-up enables Harrier to line up weapons

best areas were at the top and bottom ends of the speed range. But how does one take advantage of such characteristics, especially in light of the fact that history shows the attacker would most likely be behind you before being detected.

Considering the difficulty of starting on the defensive while attempting to integrate the unusual characteristics of the Harrier, the answers came surprisingly fast. Two of the more unique maneuvers developed to neutralize an enemy fighter who is approaching firing range are called the 'defensive break' and the 'flip'.

Describing the first in terms of pilot action required means: "When first detecting the enemy in your rear hemisphere, but not in firing range, use the brute power of the Pegasus engine to accelerate to high speed while turning to keep enough angle off to prevent the attacker from firing. If he still closes and approaches lethal range, perform a 'defensive break'. That is, pull to maximum turn rate and use a large amount of VIFF."

"The Harrier will pitch into the turn by about 30°, jump vertically towards the inside of the circle and rapidly decelerate. The attacker will be forced to overshoot, and as he slides by to the outside, reverse and turn back into him. Now he is the hunted and is faced with a choice of slow fighting an airplane that can virtually stop, or trying to out accelerate the little jet. In either case his day is ruined."

The flip is: "a second method that is used to dispose of an enemy who is close in trail is to climb at a very steep angle entering the low speed environment. Some type of spiral maneuver has to be employed while climbing, to avoid becoming a stationary target. As the speed further decays, pull the airplane through the vertical using light stick forces and small nozzle angles."

"The Harrier will 'flip' to a 90° nose low position. The attacker will be forced into a ballistic, semi-controlled turn over the top in an attempt to match your maneuver. As you both start back towards earth, put in full reverse thrust. The Harrier will essentially stop relative

to the attacker. With no way to prevent his acceleration, he will slide by in a rather helpless state. The rest is easy."

If you are fortunate enough to be the attacker, your task is simplified by VIFF. No longer do you have to worry about excessive closure rates. If the adversary detects you and performs his own defensive break, you can thrust vectoring to control the overshoot. His only choice is to continue his break away from you or reverse and engage in a slow speed fight. In either case you still have the advantage.

The effects of this capability are two fold. It allows you to become a more aggressive attacker and it denies a primary defensive counter to the airplane being attacked.

HEADING FOR A STANDOFF

With these maneuvers in hand, we were now ready to enter the next test phase; flights against airplanes with characteristics similar to Warsaw Pact fighters. The tests were exhaustive, consisting of several hundred sorties on

Lifting from deck of USS *Franklin D. Roosevelt* (CV-42), AV-8A (BuNo. 159242) from VMA-231 heads for practice target area during exercises in the Mediterranean Sea. *U.S. Navy photo K-116153*

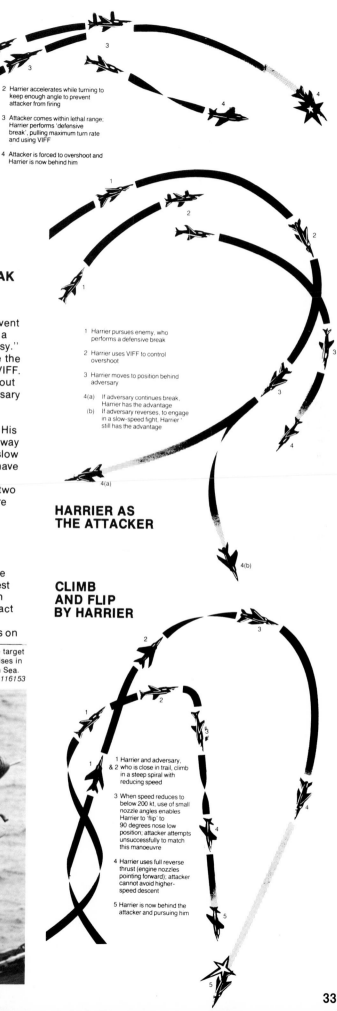

1 Enemy detected in rear hemisphere but not in firing range

2 Harrier accelerates while turning to keep enough angle to prevent attacker from firing

3 Attacker comes within lethal range; Harrier performs 'defensive break', pulling maximum turn rate and using VIFF

4 Attacker is forced to overshoot and Harrier is now behind him

DEFENSIVE BREAK BY HARRIER

1 Harrier pursues enemy, who performs a defensive break

2 Harrier uses VIFF to control overshoot

3 Harrier moves to position behind adversary

4(a) If adversary continues break, Harrier has the advantage
  (b) If adversary reverses, to engage in a slow-speed fight, Harrier still has the advantage

HARRIER AS THE ATTACKER

CLIMB AND FLIP BY HARRIER

1 Harrier and adversary, & 2 who is close in trail, climb in a steep spiral with reducing speed

3 When speed reduces to below 200 kt, use of small nozzle angles enables Harrier to 'flip' to 90 degrees nose low position; attacker attempts unsuccessfully to match this manoeuvre

4 Harrier uses full reverse thrust (engine nozzles pointing forward); attacker cannot avoid higher-speed descent

5 Harrier is now behind the attacker and pursuing him

an instrumented range. The results enthusiastically endorsed the operational effectiveness of the Harrier and in particular, the 'defensive break' and the 'flip' over the top.

Two much needed improvements were nevertheless identified by these tests: (1) an elimination of the restrictions that required the pilot to check engine parameters prior to using thrust to allow for higher vertical maneuvering against low wing loaded airplanes.

On the positive side was the fact that the much maligned endurance of the Harrier turned out to be a strong point. Although being able to carry less internal gas than most of the opponents, the fuel usage of the Pegasus engine was so much less than that required by the other jets to produce accomparable thrust to weight ratio that *they* would have to terminate the fights due to low fuel states. In peacetime tests this was not considered a big factor, but in actual combat it could prove really embarrassing to the opposition.

Overall the Harrier was impressive. We now knew that, because of thrust vectoring, the airplane could survive in a hostile air environment. However, there was still that nagging feeling that we didn't quite have our act together. There was more potential buried in the airplane and somehow we had to get at it.

THE MIRACLE COMBAT PLUG

Back to Beaufort again to work out the bugs. This time it was out of our hands though and up to the Naval Air Systems Command (NAVAIR) and the contractors

to take action. We had identified what was needed, they had to provide it.

Lo and behold, will miracles never cease. Modifications arrived to beef up the nozzle system thus eliminating most of the hated restrictions. A significant improvement but not quite all that was needed.

Then it arrived! A combat plug! A screw-in turbine temperature control fuse that allowed the engine to put out significantly more thrust when wingborne than we now had. To put this in perspective, the two minute installation of the plug resulted in a higher thrust gain than the A-4 Skyhawk had seen from all its engine improvements over a 20 year life.

The plug had one restriction and one reservation associated with its use, but they did not present an operational problem. It could only be used for 2½ minutes at a time and the effect on the life of the engine was unknown.

The 2½ minutes coincided nicely with the length of an average dogfight, and the USMC tactics of short nozzle spurts during VIFF (7 sec.) had, to date, shown no adverse effects on engine life. However, several knowledgeable people had great reservations about this latter point, not the least of which was one of the principal designers of the engine. Their thoughts had obviously influenced the deliverer of the plug, since I received it wrapped in a package marked: 'Personal, for Harry Blot only; do not reveal source; if airplane crashes while plug is installed and you get thrown clear, climb back in the fireball'. Fortunately, adventurism won out over

conservatism and NAVAIR permitted the tests to continue.

It was now time to fly the modified, plug equipped bird. It was love at first flight. The Harrier did everything that was asked of it. The airplane had crossed the line from being good to being great. This was the end of the project. All the potential was tapped. If an attacker wanted to shoot down this airplane, he was going to have to earn his hero medal.

The raw power allowed you to pitch vertically high enough to make the pilot of a low wing loaded airplane commit himself to a turn direction, thus enabling you to flip back at him, accelerate to gun range before he could escape and get in a good shot. No longer was it necessary to look into the cockpit to check gauges. You could concentrate on the target.

A FIRST RATE FIGHTER

Further tests were conducted to verify the capability of the modified bird and verify they did! There was no longer any question about what it would do when all the deficiencies were corrected. The Harrier's ACM capability was absolutely eye watering!

Several significant results come from these trials. First, the Harrier evolved from a barely survivable attack airplane to an airplane that could not only survive, but stood an excellent chance of destroying its attacker. Secondly, thrust vectoring was proven to be a valuable, operationally significant means of enhancing the characteristics of a tactical airplane. Finally, the improvements needed to optimize the use of thrust vectoring in air combat were identified for future use.

Aircraft maintenance men perform preflight check on AV-8A during 1976 Mediterranean Sea exercises on board carrier *USS Franklin D. Roosevelt* (CV-42). Note large size of port-intake-mounted inflight refueling probe. *U.S. Navy photo 1168905 by Greg Haas*

Direct head-on view of AV-8A mounting two ADEN cannon and two LAU-68 2.75" rocket pods. Extensive throat area of intakes is readily apparent. *Aerophile photo*

Direct aft view of AV-8A illustrates extreme anhedral of both wing and slab stabilator. *Aerophile*

VMA-513 AV-8A (BuNo. 158976) during static display at Japanese airshow. *Toshiki Kudo photo*

Two AV-8A's approach the aft deck of the *USS Guam* (LPH-9) during Mediterranean Cruise flight operations. *U.S. Marine Corps photo 452540*

Mid-1975 saw this Harrier of VMA-231 (BuNo159238) taking off from Landing Zone Dove during Operation "Solid Shield." The site of the exercise was Camp Lejeune, North Carolina. *U.S. Marine Corps photo A142971 by Bob Marshall*

An aircraft maintenance man uses a towing tractor to move an AV-8A across the deck of the carrier *USS Franklin D. Roosevelt* (CV-42) during 1976 exercises in the Mediterranean Sea. *U.S. Navy photo 1168904 by Greg Haas*

It is difficult to tell, from a still photo, whether an AV-8 is landing or taking off. All external clues are the same under either circumstance. Here, however, a VMA-231 AV-8A (BuNo. 159246) hovers during landing on board carrier *USS Franklin D. Roosevelt* (CV-42). *U.S. Navy photo 1168911 by Greg Haas*

Another distinct advantage the AV-8 has over conventional aircraft is its ability to utilize a takeoff technique now referred to as "ski jump". In this concept, the ship deck from which STO is accomplished is not flat, but raised for the last 100 feet or so, thus providing the aircraft with a ballistic trajectory as it leaves the deck. Currently the Navy is studying ship designs that will feature ski jumps with 100 foot circular arcs and exit angles of up to 12-degrees.

Because the aircraft has a ballistic trajectory, it can leave the deck at a lower speed than would be necessary with a flat deck. Speed is built up during the ballistic portion of the flight until the aircraft attains normal wingborne flight. This provides several benefits, which may be any of the following or some combination of them:

1. For a given takeoff weight, the STO deck run is shorter than with a flat deck (STO's could be performed on shorter, smaller ships.)

2. For a given deck run, the takeoff weight is increased, thus increasing the useable payload.

3. For certain takeoffs, the ship need not steam at high speed because the ski jump provides an effect equivalent to an additional WOD. (An economy in ship fuel is possible.)

4. The aircraft can leave the ski jump at any point in the ship's pitching cycle because the upward trajectory cancels the effects of the bow-down part of the cycle. Further, this is virtually independent of the amplitude of the deck motion (within the constraints of practical aircraft deck handling).

Tests of the ski jump/Harrier combination have been carried out in Britain using exit angles as high as 20-degrees. These tests have demonstrated that the potential benefits of the ski jump are realizable. A 15-degree to 20-degree ramp will provide at least a 2,500 pound increase in launch weight compared to a flat deck STO, in typical ship operating conditions. Alternatively for a given launch weight, a 15-degree to 20-degree ski jump launch requires only half the corresponding flat deck run. Further, no handling problems have occurred even in mistrimmed launches, in launches with auto stabilizers off, in launches with over 15 knot crosswind, and when the pilot was "blinded" under screens in the rear cockpit of the two-seat AV-8.

The ramp used at the Farnborough Air Show in 1978 has been installed at the Naval Air Test Center, Patuxent River, Maryland. This ramp is being used for U.S. tests of the ski jump concept and is expected to result in the incorporation of such ramps onboard operational U.S. combat ships in the near future.

YAV-8B No. 1 (BuNo 158394) tries its hand at the ski-jump assisted short take-off. *McDonnell Douglas photo C12-8070-2*

AV-8A (BuNo. 158975) in VMA-513 markings prepares for takeoff. Rudder is blue with white stars. *McDonnell Douglas photo*

GENERAL
Description

AV-8A/TAV-8A

FUSELAGE: is a conventional semi-monocoque safe-life aluminum structure of frames and stringers. Titanium skin is used at the rear and around engine exhaust and high temp areas. Access to the engine is through a large opening at the top of the fuselage, ahead of the wing center section. Reaction control valves for pitch and yaw are located in the nose and extended tailcone. There is a large, hydraulically actuated forward-hinged airbrake under the fuselage, aft of the main wheel well.

WING: is a cantilever shoulder type with a wing section developed by British Aerospace (Hawker Siddeley). Thickness/chord ratio is 10% at the root and 5% at the tip. Anhedral is 12-degrees. Incidence is 1-degree 45-minutes. Sweepback at quarter chord is 34-degrees. Basic structure is a one-piece aluminum alloy three-spar design with integrally-machined skins, manufactured by Brough factory of British Aerospace. Attachment to the fuselage occurs at six points via bolts. Roll control is via conventional ailerons which are hydraulically actuated. There are also electro-hydraulically operated trailing edge flaps, one located on each wing and controlled by a common hydraulic actuator. Both flaps and ailerons are of bonded aluminum alloy honeycomb construction. The ailerons are irreversible. Jet reaction control units, for roll control during low and zero speed flight are located in front of each outrigger wheel fairing. For ferry missions, the normal wingtips can be replaced by bolt-on extended tips offering improved aspect ratio and lower drag.

TAIL UNIT: consists of a one-piece variable-incidence slab stabilator with 15-degrees of anhedral, irreversibly actuated by a Fairey tandem hydraulic jack. Rudder and trailing edge of stabilator are of bonded aluminum honeycomb construction. The rudder is manually operated and has no boost. There is a trim tab on the rudder. A ventral fin for improved directional control at high angles of attack is mounted under the rear fuselage and contains a faired VHF antenna.

POWERPLANT: The AV-8 is powered by a Rolls Royce (Bristol Division) F402-RR-402 twin spool, axial flow, turbofan engine with a nominal bypass ratio of 1.38 and an overall nominal cycle pressure ratio of 13.7. It has thrust vectoring exhaust nozzles which can be vectored from straight aft, down through 98.5-degrees. The fan contains three stages, which supply cold air to the forward two exhaust nozzles, and is powered by a 2-stage low-pressure turbine. There is also an 8-stage high pressure compressor driven by a two-stage high pressure turbine. Each spool is independent of the other, but they are co-axial and, to minimize gyroscopic effect, they contra-rotate. The engine, with water injection providing thrust boosting, develops a nominal (static test bed) thrust of 21,500

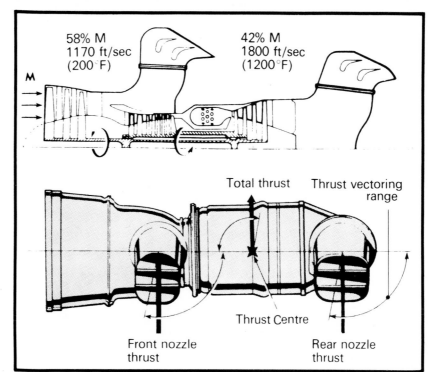

VECTORED-THRUST POWERPLANT

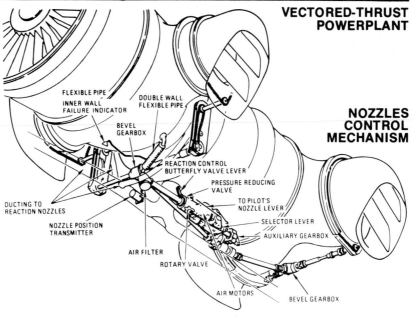

NOZZLES CONTROL MECHANISM

DESCRIPTION	AV-8A POWER PLANT
Model Number	F402-RR-402 (Pegasus 11)
Manufacturer	Rolls-Royce
Type	Axial Flow, Nonmixed Vectored Thrust, Turbofan
Augmentation	Water Injection
Length (including nozzles)	140.9 in.
Case Diameter	48.05 in.
Width (across forward nozzles)	96.42 in.
Airflow @ 100% RPM (SLSDS)	430.7 LB/SEC
Dry Weight	3653 lb.
Nozzle Rotation Angles	0° to 98.5°

POWER SETTING (TIME)	MINIMUM ENGINE UNINSTALLED THRUST SLS*	ENGINE SPEED (RPM)
Short Lift Wet** (15 sec)	20,930	106.8%
Normal Lift Wet** (2.5 Min)	20,395	104.1%
Short Lift Dry (15 Sec)	19,920	102.7%
Normal Lift Dry (2.5 Min)	19,020	100.0%
Maximum (15 Min)	16,350	94.4%
Maximum Continuous	13,100	88.0%
Idle	1,000	27.0%

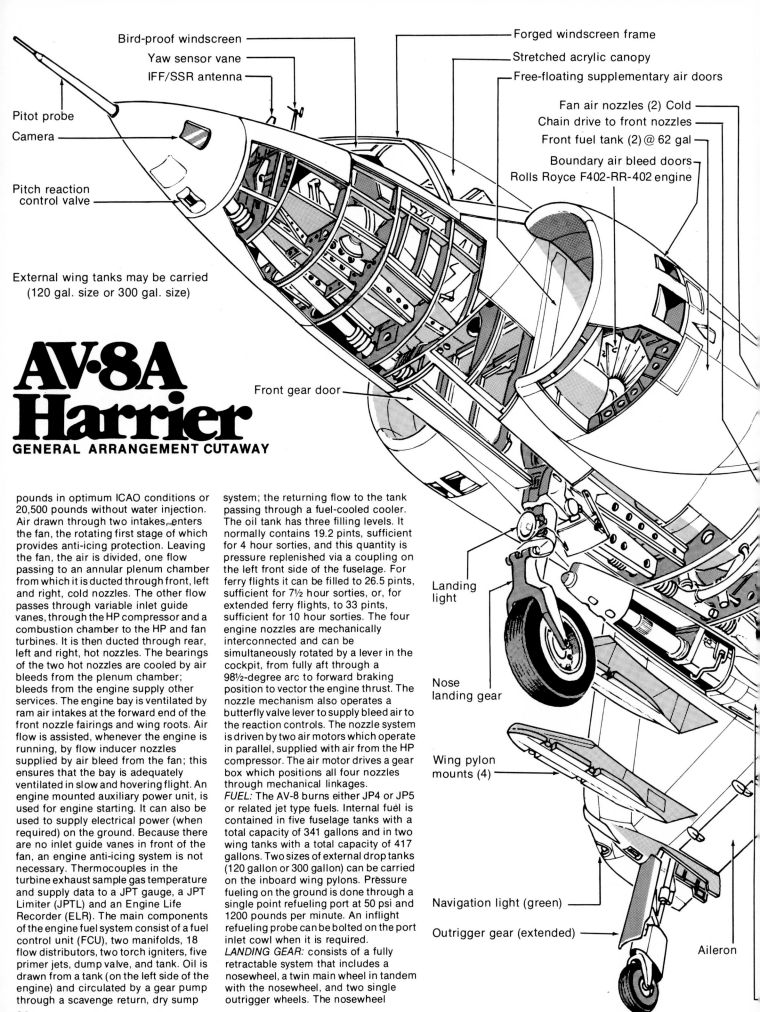

Bird-proof windscreen

Yaw sensor vane

IFF/SSR antenna

Pitot probe

Camera

Pitch reaction control valve

External wing tanks may be carried (120 gal. size or 300 gal. size)

Forged windscreen frame

Stretched acrylic canopy

Free-floating supplementary air doors

Fan air nozzles (2) Cold

Chain drive to front nozzles

Front fuel tank (2) @ 62 gal

Boundary air bleed doors

Rolls Royce F402-RR-402 engine

AV·8A Harrier
GENERAL ARRANGEMENT CUTAWAY

Front gear door

Landing light

Nose landing gear

Wing pylon mounts (4)

Navigation light (green)

Outrigger gear (extended)

Aileron

pounds in optimum ICAO conditions or 20,500 pounds without water injection. Air drawn through two intakes, enters the fan, the rotating first stage of which provides anti-icing protection. Leaving the fan, the air is divided, one flow passing to an annular plenum chamber from which it is ducted through front, left and right, cold nozzles. The other flow passes through variable inlet guide vanes, through the HP compressor and a combustion chamber to the HP and fan turbines. It is then ducted through rear, left and right, hot nozzles. The bearings of the two hot nozzles are cooled by air bleeds from the plenum chamber; bleeds from the engine supply other services. The engine bay is ventilated by ram air intakes at the forward end of the front nozzle fairings and wing roots. Air flow is assisted, whenever the engine is running, by flow inducer nozzles supplied by air bleed from the fan; this ensures that the bay is adequately ventilated in slow and hovering flight. An engine mounted auxiliary power unit, is used for engine starting. It can also be used to supply electrical power (when required) on the ground. Because there are no inlet guide vanes in front of the fan, an engine anti-icing system is not necessary. Thermocouples in the turbine exhaust sample gas temperature and supply data to a JPT gauge, a JPT Limiter (JPTL) and an Engine Life Recorder (ELR). The main components of the engine fuel system consist of a fuel control unit (FCU), two manifolds, 18 flow distributors, two torch igniters, five primer jets, dump valve, and tank. Oil is drawn from a tank (on the left side of the engine) and circulated by a gear pump through a scavenge return, dry sump

system; the returning flow to the tank passing through a fuel-cooled cooler. The oil tank has three filling levels. It normally contains 19.2 pints, sufficient for 4 hour sorties, and this quantity is pressure replenished via a coupling on the left front side of the fuselage. For ferry flights it can be filled to 26.5 pints, sufficient for 7½ hour sorties, or, for extended ferry flights, to 33 pints, sufficient for 10 hour sorties. The four engine nozzles are mechanically interconnected and can be simultaneously rotated by a lever in the cockpit, from fully aft through a 98½-degree arc to forward braking position to vector the engine thrust. The nozzle mechanism also operates a butterfly valve lever to supply bleed air to the reaction controls. The nozzle system is driven by two air motors which operate in parallel, supplied with air from the HP compressor. The air motor drives a gear box which positions all four nozzles through mechanical linkages.

FUEL: The AV-8 burns either JP4 or JP5 or related jet type fuels. Internal fuel is contained in five fuselage tanks with a total capacity of 341 gallons and in two wing tanks with a total capacity of 417 gallons. Two sizes of external drop tanks (120 gallon or 300 gallon) can be carried on the inboard wing pylons. Pressure fueling on the ground is done through a single point refueling port at 50 psi and 1200 pounds per minute. An inflight refueling probe can be bolted on the port inlet cowl when it is required.

LANDING GEAR: consists of a fully retractable system that includes a nosewheel, a twin main wheel in tandem with the nosewheel, and two single outrigger wheels. The nosewheel retracts forward while the main wheels retract aft into fuselage bays. The outrigger wheels retract aft and are partially enclosed in a fairing assembly just inboard of the wingtips. The landing gear is electrically controlled by the main 28 volt dc bus, and actuated by the No. 1 hydraulic system. Accidental retraction of the landing gear when the aircraft is on the ground is prevented by a scissor switch on the main gear, and ground safety locks. When the main gear is retracted, the fuselage bay is enclosed by flush fitting doors. These doors are mechanically connected to the main gear to open and close on gear retraction and extension. The landing gear are manufactured by Dowty Rotol and permit operation from rough, unprepared surfaces of CBR as low as 3 to 5 percent. There is a nitrogen bottle provided for emergency inflight extension. The nosewheel leg is of levered-suspension liquid spring type. The outrigger gear are of the telescopic oleo-pneumatic type, as are the mains.

Dunlop wheels and tires normally equip the AV-8, these being as follows: nosewheel 26 x 8.75-11 at 90 psi; mainwheels 27 x 7.74-13 at 95 psi; and outrigger wheels 13.50 x 6.4 at 95 psi. The nosewheel steering system is an electro-hydraulic operated system that provides directional control for ground operations in three modes: steer, castor, and center. The steering mode has a range of 45-degrees left and right of rudder pedal center. The castor mode has a range of 179-degrees left or right.

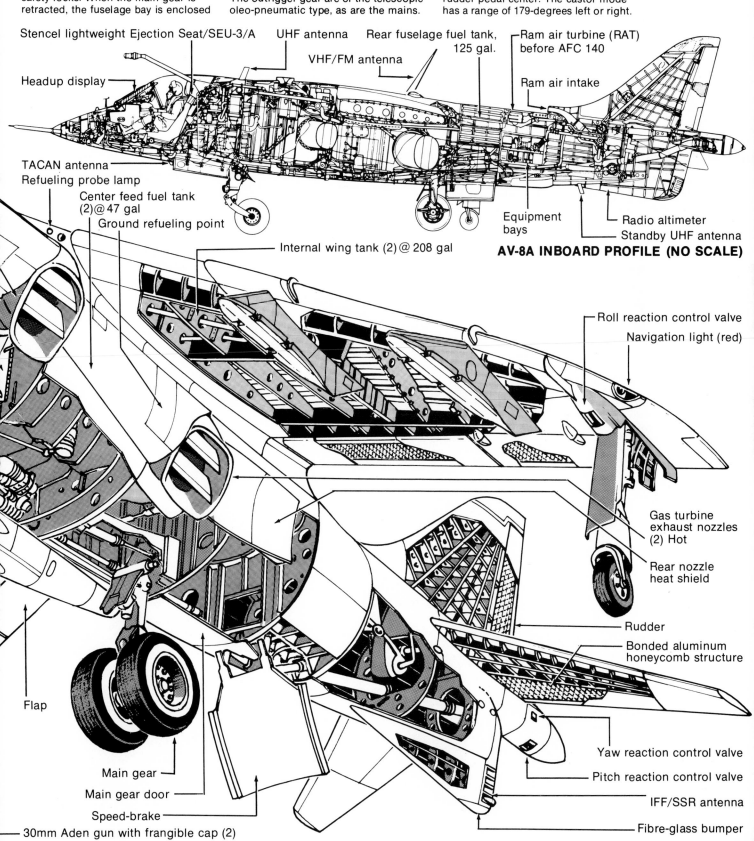

Stencel lightweight Ejection Seat/SEU-3/A
UHF antenna
Rear fuselage fuel tank, 125 gal.
Ram air turbine (RAT) before AFC 140
VHF/FM antenna
Ram air intake
Headup display
TACAN antenna
Refueling probe lamp
Center feed fuel tank (2)@ 47 gal
Ground refueling point
Equipment bays
Radio altimeter
Standby UHF antenna
Internal wing tank (2) @ 208 gal

AV-8A INBOARD PROFILE (NO SCALE)

Roll reaction control valve
Navigation light (red)
Gas turbine exhaust nozzles (2) Hot
Rear nozzle heat shield
Rudder
Bonded aluminum honeycomb structure
Flap
Main gear
Main gear door
Speed-brake
30mm Aden gun with frangible cap (2)
Yaw reaction control valve
Pitch reaction control valve
IFF/SSR antenna
Fibre-glass bumper

39

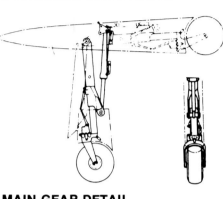

Front, side and 3/4 rear views of balancing gear mounted near AV-8A wingtip. Gear retracts rearward and wheel and tire are left exposed to slipstream — though they are faired into strut and create little parasitic drag. Note tiedown ring about half-way down main strut. *Aerophile photo*

OUTRIGGER GEAR DETAIL

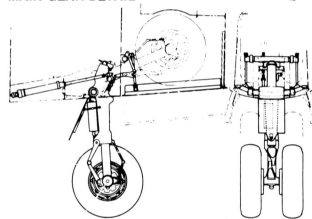

Knuckle type nose gear of AV-8A is steerable and retracts forward. Also visible in this photo is retractable cockpit entrance and egress step. Note landing light mounted just above gear knuckle. *Aerophile photo*

MAIN GEAR DETAIL

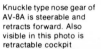

Rear view of AV-8A main landing gear. Hydraulically actuated disc brakes are mounted inside strut-side of wheels. Note short length of main strut. *Aerophile photo*

Main gear of AV-8A is compact and relatively lightweight. Gear retracts rearward into fuselage well. *Aerophile photo*

NOSE GEAR DETAIL

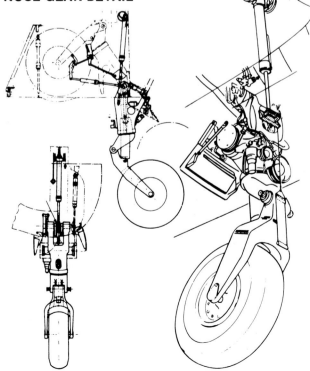

Forward exhaust nozzles rotate slightly past 90-degrees to centerline. Nozzle is illustrated in its direct-aft setting for conventional horizontal flight. Note that nozzle has divider plates optimized for smoothing exhaust flow pattern. Note, also, nozzle fairing to right of photo. *Aerophile photo*

Close-up detail of AV-8A ventral airbrake. Hydraulic actuating piston is just visible immediately under fuselage opening. *Aerophile photo*

View down the throat of AV-8A intake gives good illustration of Rolls Royce Pegasus first fan stage. Note boundary layer bleed door in closed position on the right. Barely visible on bottom of intake lip is "no step" symbol. *Aerophile photo*

Rolls Royce Pegasus removal requires that the entire wing be separated from the Harrier's fuselage. This is relatively easy to accomplish and can be done in the field with the right equipment. Note exhaust ports on engine sides. Pegasus is a stubby, lightweight power-plant with an exceptional thrust-to-weight ratio. Note unusual markings of this AV-8A (BuNo. 158703). Vertical fin is painted orange. *Rolls Royce photo*

BRAKE SYSTEM: The twin-wheel main landing gear is equipped with Dunlop hydraulically operated disc brakes. The brakes operate simultaneously and progressively as either brake pedal is depressed. Cables from each brake pedal and the brake lock lever are attached to a lever box. A common cable connects the lever box to a brake control valve. An anti-skid system and parking brake are also incorporated into the normal brake system. A nitrogen charged accumulator provides sufficient hydraulic pressure for normal and anti-skid braking if PC-1 pressure is not available. Two hydraulic pressure indicators located on the left console, provide brake accumulator pressure, and applied brake pressure. The brake accumulator indicator has a range from 0 to 4, multiplied by 1000. The brake pressure indicator has a range from 0 to 2, multiplied by 1000. If excessive heating occurs in a main wheel, a fusible plug melts and the tire will deflate.

LIGHTING: consists of instrument and general interior lighting and exterior lighting consisting of navigation lights, anti-collision lights, landing lights, and an air-to-air refueling light.

COCKPIT: is an enclosed, pressurized (3.5 psi), climate controlled area, that contains a vertically adjustable ejection seat (which see). The main instrument panel is arranged to receive the attitude heading reference system and ballistic selection panel in the center of the panel. Also contained in the center, are warning lights and navigational aids. On the left side are the armament and missile control panels, in addition to the flight information indicators. The right side contains primarily engine operating indicators. The left console is provided with flight control, landing gear position indicators, throttle and nozzle quadrant and pressure indicators. The power reset and engine start switches, communication control panels, oxygen indicators, and anti-G suit control valves are located on the right console. The cockpit is also provided with a warning/caution lights panel to alert the pilot for immediate action and for advisory warnings.

AIR CONDITIONING AND PRESSURIZATION SYSTEM: includes cockpit air conditioning and pressurization, canopy sealing, windshield/camera window washing, equipment air conditioning, and anti-G suit pressurization. These systems are powered by sixth stage engine high pressure compressor bleed air.

EJECTION SEAT: The AV-8A and TAV-8A are equipped with a Stencel SEU-3/A ejection seat which utilizes catapult and rocket thrust to propel it from the aircraft. The SEU-3/A provides escape capability during takeoff and landing emergencies at zero speeds, zero altitude, and throughout the remainder of the flight envelope of the airplane, except for very unusual flight conditions. It incorporates a seat mounted personnel parachute and accommodates a survival package with a pararaft, and is designed for use with an integrated torso harness. An emergency oxygen supply and an emergency locator beacon are provided. A non-adjustable headrest is part of the seat structure and houses the face curtain and seat mounted parachute. The front surface of the seat bucket serves as a buffer for the calves of the legs. The sides of the bucket extend forward to protect the legs and a leg restraint system is incorporated to prevent flailing during high speed ejection. The ejection sequence is

ROLLS-ROYCE LIMITED

BRITISH AEROSPACE

Noteworthy details in this cockpit view include the HUD, instrument panel and stick. *Aerophile*

Detail close-up of forward engine exhaust nozzle, and forward nozzle fairing. *Aerophile photo*

Cramped interior of the Harrier's cockpit is apparent in this wide-angle view. *Aerophile*

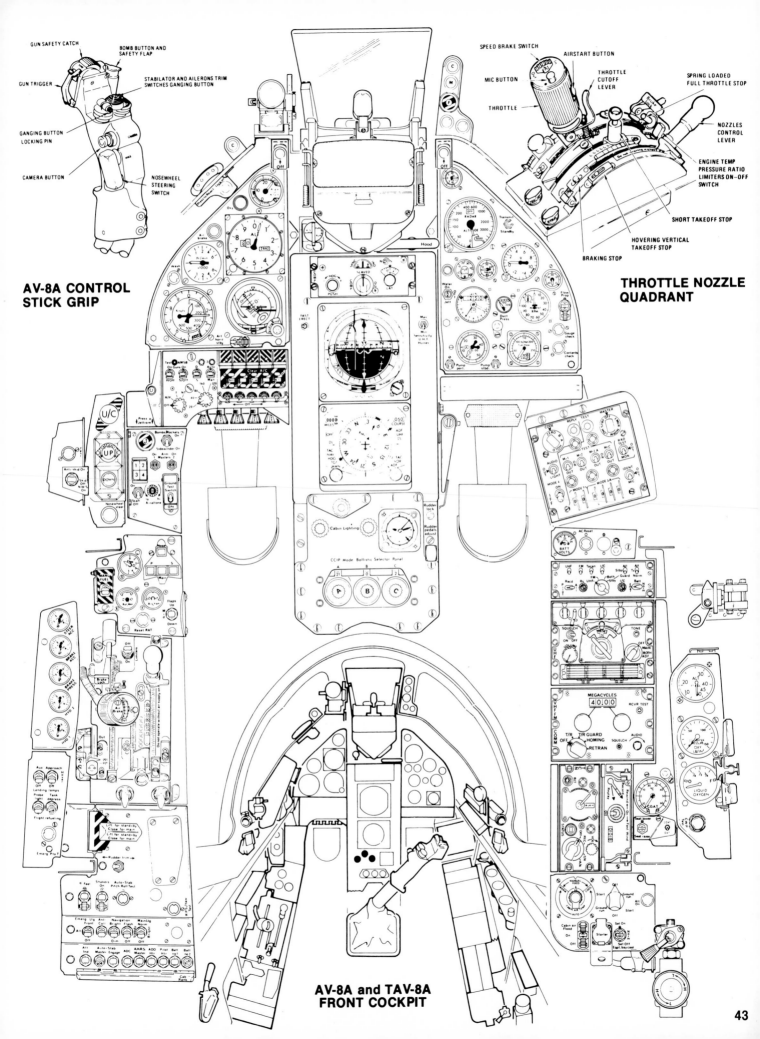

AV-8A CONTROL STICK GRIP

GUN SAFETY CATCH
BOMB BUTTON AND SAFETY FLAP
GUN TRIGGER
STABILATOR AND AILERONS TRIM SWITCHES GANGING BUTTON
GANGING BUTTON LOCKING PIN
CAMERA BUTTON
NOSEWHEEL STEERING SWITCH

THROTTLE NOZZLE QUADRANT

SPEED BRAKE SWITCH
AIRSTART BUTTON
MIC BUTTON
THROTTLE CUTOFF LEVER
SPRING LOADED FULL THROTTLE STOP
THROTTLE
NOZZLES CONTROL LEVER
ENGINE TEMP PRESSURE RATIO LIMITERS ON—OFF SWITCH
SHORT TAKEOFF STOP
HOVERING VERTICAL TAKEOFF STOP
BRAKING STOP

AV-8A and TAV-8A FRONT COCKPIT

initiated by pulling the face curtain handle with both hands. The sequence may also be initiated by pulling the lower ejection handle. Full travel of the face curtain or lower ejection handle fires the ejection seat initiators which in turn fire four ejection seat catapult cartridge igniters, igniting the catapult cartridge to eject the seat. The ejection seat initiators also ignite the shoulder harness gas generator, a dual time-delay unit, and a miniature detonating cord (MDC) thruster. The MDC thruster initiates canopy shattering and removes the airspeed sensor and autotone arming keys. As the seat and outer catapult tubes travel upward the emergency oxygen and emergency locator beacon (AN/URT-33) systems are activated, the leg restraint lines are pulled tight to restrain the legs against the front of the seat pan, and the personnel services connector block is disconnected. After approximately 22 inches of seat travel a gas port is opened allowing gas pressure to act upon the base of a drogue gun, housed within the catapult assemblies, ejecting a drogue parachute and its container from the seat. Gas pressure is also directed to a time-delay initiator and two seat back rockets (SBR). The SBR are ignited to provide the momentum necessary for man/seat combination to attain sufficient terrain clearance to permit parachute deployment. Seat stabilization, upon ejection, is controlled by the directional automatic realignment of trajectory (DART) system by the

means of lanyards attached between the seat and aircraft feeding through tension brake assemblies to counteract excessive pitch and roll conditions. A post ejection sequence system is capable of four modes of operation, depending on ejection airspeed and altitude. An emergency release control handle, when activated, released the pilot from the seat for emergency egress while on the ground, and provides for manual man/seat separation and personnel parachute deployment after ejection. A survival package release handle provides manual deployment of the survival package.

CANOPY SYSTEM: The cockpit area is enclosed by a sliding type canopy which consists of a shell molded from a single piece of transparent plastic and mounted in a metal frame. The canopy is mounted on rails which slope upward toward the rear of the aircraft. The canopy is pre-loaded to the open position by an elastic cord and pulley system. A canopy opening brake is encountered by the canopy before it is fully opened. The brake dissipates the initial momentum imparted by the elastic cords. Except for the aid provided by the elastic and cord pre-load, the canopy is normally opened and closed manually without hydraulic or pneumatic boost. The canopy operating mechanism is

mechanically linked to a boarding step on the right forward fuselage so that as the canopy opens the step extends and as the canopy closes, the step retracts. When moved to the fully closed position, the canopy is automatically locked by two latches at the intersection of the lower leading edge of the canopy bow and the windshield frame. Each lock has an associated locking indicator in the cockpit. External and internal controls are provided for both normal and emergency operation. Release handles unlock the canopy and the canopy bow handles are used as grips to open and close it. Once locked externally, the canopy can be opened and closed by means of the boarding step. Emergency operation of the canopy consists of detonating a small explosive charge of miniature detonating cord (MDC) which serves to break away or shatter the molded plastic shell. The MDC is a thin explosive cord attached around the edge of the plastic shell near the canopy frame and also looped around the center of the canopy just above the pilot's helmet. A canopy seal, routed over the canopy sills and around the windshield arch, is automatically inflated by a solenoid operated pneumatic valve whenever the aircraft becomes airborne.

AVIONICS AND INSTRUMENTATION: Basic instrument compliments consist

Difficult to photograph details are clearly defined in this view of a Harrier's ejection seat. *Aerophile*

SEU-3/A EJECTION SEAT

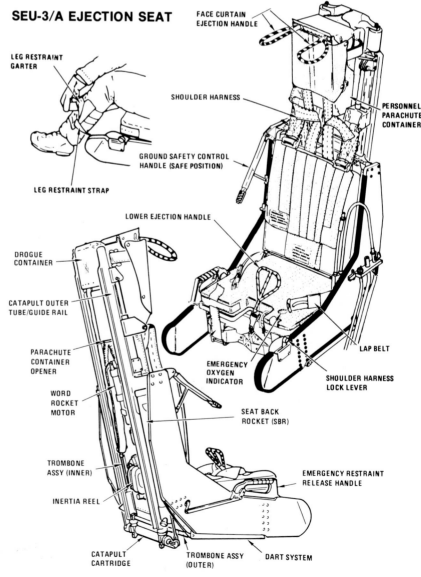

of the following items: altimeter, radar altimeter set (AN/APN-194), radar altitude indicator, airspeed indicator, vertical velocity indicator, standby attitude indicator, standby compass, angle of attack indicator and associated probe, accelerometer, and an elapsed time indicator. There is also a Sperry C2G compass, a Smiths electronic head up display of flight information and a Smiths air data computer. The INAS can be aligned at sea or on land. The weapon aiming computer provides a general solution for manual or automatic release of freefall and related bombs, and for the aiming of rockets and guns, in dive and straight-pass attacks over a wide range of flight conditions and very considerable freedom of maneuver in elevation. Laser rangefinding and target seeker units are also adaptable to the AV-8 weapons system.

COMMUNICATION NAVIGATION IDENTIFICATION (CNI) EQUIPMENT: consists of a communication control panel, a ground intercom, a main UHF system, a standby UHF system, a UHF homer, a VHF (FM) system, an identification (IFF) system, and a tacan set.

Communication controls — contains the switches and knobs for operation of the communication systems.
Ground Intercommunication — there are three on the aircraft. They are located at the rear of the right console, at the rear of the equipment bay, and behind a spring-loaded access door on the left front nozzle fairing.
UHF Communication System — provides air-to-air or air-to-ground radio communication and homing facilities in the UHF range, 225.0 to

399.95 MHz. The system provides line of sight transmission and reception range of approximately 250 miles from air-to-ground, and 550 miles from air-to-air, depending on the altitude. The system operates on 3,500 channels spaced 50 kHz apart with a capability for 20 preset channels, plus a separate guard channel.
UHF Homer — is brought into operation when the function selector knob is placed to the ADF position, and either the UHF receiver audio switch or the function selector knob on the communication control panel is set to the UHF position.
VHF (FM) Communication System — provides communication in the VHF frequency range of 30.00 to 75.95 MHz. The system contains a main receiver and transitter, a fix-tuned

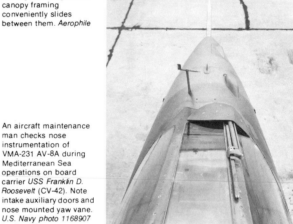

Front windscreen, yaw indicating vane, and windscreen wiper are shown in this unusual view facing forward from the cockpit of an AV-8A. *Aerophile photo*

Detail of opened canopy rear section. Note that small segment of intake lip is attached to canopy framework. UHF antenna protrude from top of fuselage and segment of canopy framing conveniently slides between them. *Aerophile*

Interesting head-on shot shows flight crewmen spotting an AV-8A on the flight deck of the carrier *USS Franklin D. Roosevelt* (CV-42). *U.S. Navy photo 1168920 by Greg Haas*

An aircraft maintenance man checks nose instrumentation of VMA-231 AV-8A during Mediterranean Sea operations on board carrier *USS Franklin D. Roosevelt* (CV-42). Note intake auxiliary doors and nose mounted yaw vane. *U.S. Navy photo 1168907 by Greg Haas*

guard receiver, and has a homing capability (which is presently not used).

TACAN System — operates in conjunction with a tacan ground or airborne beacon for navigational purposes. The system provides an indication of the position of the aircraft relative to the beacon by a display of range and bearing information on the tacan indicator.

Identification System — provides automatic identification of the aircraft when challenged by an IFF (military) or SSR (civil secondary surveillance radar) ground radar system. In response to interrogation signals, the system also provides coded altitude data derived from the air data computer, and coded emergency signals. The coded emergency signals are transmitted automatically if the seat is ejected from the aircraft.

PITOT-STATIC SYSTEM: pitot-static pressures are obtained from the pitot-static head on the nose boom and are furnished to the pitot-static operated flight instruments, air data computer, rudder pedal shaker airspeed switch, Q feel control unit, and the ejection seat airspeed sensor.

AIR DATA COMPUTER: receives inputs from the pitot-static system and the total temperature probe and furnishes the following outputs: a. Engine pressure ratio limiter — 10,000 feet altitude signal; b. Aileron stop solenoid — 250 knots IAS signal; c. IFF — pressure altitude; d. I/WAC — pressure altitude, IAS, and TAS; e. Head-up display — Pressure altitude, IAS, TAS, and Mach; f. Wheels warning light — 165 knots; g. Q-feel — 250 knot IAS signal.

HUD: enables the pilot to see in his normal head-up field of view the symbols traced out on the CRT. The unit consists of a 2'' diameter cathode ray tube (CRT),

Marine Corps pilot extricates himself from the cramped quarters of his Harrier. Photo was shot during Air Fiesta at Randolph A.F.B. in May, 1980. *Aerophile photo*

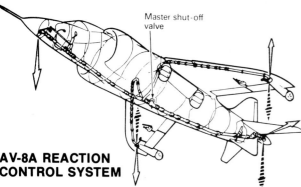

AV-8A REACTION CONTROL SYSTEM

Master shut-off valve

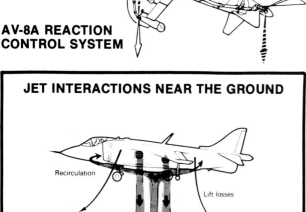

JET INTERACTIONS NEAR THE GROUND

Recirculation

Jet pumping action

Lift losses

Ground erosion

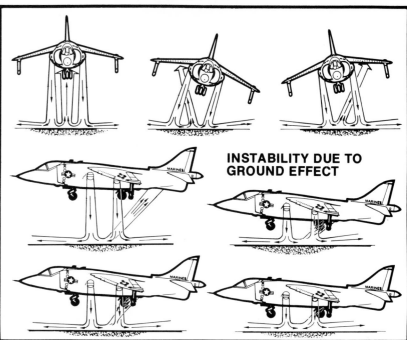

INSTABILITY DUE TO GROUND EFFECT

Evaluation of the AV-8A continued in March 1972 as this Harrier landed on the run-way set up at Landing Zone Goose at Camp Lejeune. This was during Exercise "Versatile Warrior". *U.S. Marine Corps photo A451418 by A.M. Bell*

collimating lens and mirror system for projecting the CRT imagery onto the HUD combining glass, and a reflector and reflector drive servo mechanism. There is also a HUD camera that records the picture of the field of vision ahead of the aircraft with the HUD symbols superimposed.

REACTION CONTROLS: provide control, when jetborne, by reaction valves strategically placed around the moment arm points of the airplane. The reaction valves are shutter valves supplied with bleed air ducted from the HP compressor, via a master butterfly valve which is interconnected with the engine nozzles control mechanism by a valve lever. Duct pressure is shown on a gauge in the cockpit. The master butterfly valve opens automatically when the nozzles are deflected from fully aft. Air supply is progressive over the engine nozzle range of 0-degrees to approximately 20-degrees down, thereafter maximum airflow is provided.

STABILITY AUGMENTATION SYSTEM: provides assistance in maintaining stability during hover and transitional flight by sensing movements about the pitch, roll and yaw axes of the aircraft

AV-8A (BuNo. 158956) of VMA-542 serves to illustrate empennage configuration of Harrier. Note dialectic paneling at tip and lower portion of vertical fin, and similar dialectic paneling making up a considerable portion of the ventral fin surface area. Also note break in leading edge of slab stabilator and hard rubber bumper at base of ventral fin. Rear puffer tailcone, for yaw control at low speeds, is rectangular cut-out between two round holes. *Aerophile photo*

Relatively high-altitude hover by VMA-513 AV-8A (BuNo. 158977) again illustrates nose-high attitude of type during hover, angle of exhaust nozzles, and extended airbrake. Note that belly of AV-8A was painted all-white. *Aerophile photo*

Landing approach of VMA-231 AV-8A (BuNo. 159253) shows airplane in hover with nozzles rotated to 90-degrees, gear deployed, airbrake extended, and intake doors in open position. *Rolls Royce photo*

and initiating a controlled reaction to oppose the initial movement, thus augmenting the pilot's demands to the control surface and/or reaction control valves. A pitch/roll sub-system, provides the stability augmentation in the pitch and roll axes of the aircraft, while a yaw sub-system provides the augmentation in the yaw axis.

OXYGEN SYSTEM: consists of a five liter vacuum insulated container, build-up coil, check and vent valves, pressure and quantity gauges, man-mounted regulator, and mask. The system delivers gaseous oxygen to the regulator at a nominal pressure of 60 to 90 psi. If delivery pressure falls below 45 to 50 psi, the OXY light on the warning light panel will illuminate.

ELECTRICAL POWER SUPPLY SYSTEM: consists of a primary ac electrical system powered by a single generator, a secondary dc electrical system composed of a dc transformer-rectifier for conversion of ac to dc, a power distribution (bus) system, a Lucas auxiliary power unit (apu) generator, and a receptacle for plugging in external power. Three 25 volt 25 Ah batteries are included. Two of the batteries are used to smooth out operation of the transfomer-rectifier and for use when the transformer-rectifier is inoperative. The third battery is for emergency use. The generator supplies ac power to the 115/200 volt ac bus and the transformer-rectifier. The transformer-rectifier converts 115/200

volt ac power to 28 volt dc power, which is supplied to the main 28 volt bus, the alert 28 volt dc bus, the No. 1 and No. 2 battery buses, and the No. 1 and No. 2 armament buses.

HYDRAULIC POWER SUPPLY SYSTEM: consists of two separate and independent hydraulic systems. The systems are the power and control system one (PC-1) and the power and control system two (PC-2). Both systems operate at 3,000 + or - 200 psi (nominal) and each system contains an engine driven pump, reservoir and flight control accumulators. On aircraft before AFC 140, an emergency system (RAT) is interconnected with the PC-2 system. Aircraft after AFC 140 do not have a ram air turbine. The hydraulic accumulators in each system also provide an emergency supply for short periods and prevent momentary pressure drops due to hydraulic surges. If a failure occurs in one system, the remaining system is capable of providing the back up.

WEAPON SYSTEM: consists of a bomb release system, a gun firing system, the HUD, and air-to-air-missile system. These are as follows:

1. The bomb release system consists of weapon controls in the cockpit, suspension equipment required for carrying the bombs/rockets, and

control circuits for releasing/firing the weapons. The primary weapon release controls are on the weapon control panel, the Sidewinder control panel, and the control stick. These controls enable the pilot to select and arm specific weapons, establish a release sequence, and release/fire the selected weapon. Suspension equipment for carrying weapons may be installed on five non-jettisonable pylons.

2. The gun firing system consists of two non-jettisonable 30mm gun pods which may be installed on the lower sides of the fuselage. Each gun pod may be loaded with 130 rounds of ammunition and utilized for air-to-ground or air-to-air gunnery. Gun aiming symbols are presented on the HUD combining glass. Controls required for operating the guns consist of the gun selector switches on the weapon control panel and the gun trigger and safety

Single point refueling of an AV-8A by Air Force personnel at Bergstrom AFB. *Aerophile*

Large drop tank size is apparent in this photo. Two sizes are available (120 and 300 gal.). Visible near top of leading edge of wing are vortex generators for improved chord-wise slipstream control at low speeds. Note small wing fences and hefty wing pylons. *Aerophile photo*

VMA-513 AV-8A (BuNo. 158392) sits following landing at Randolph AFB, Texas. Note LAU-68 2.75'' rocket pods and extended RAT (Ram Air Turbine). The latter provides emergency hydraulic power for controls and landing gear extension in case main systems fail. *Aerophile photo*

The Ram Air Turbine (RAT) in extended position. *George Cockle photo*

catch on the control stick.

3. The HUD system obtains information from various AHRS/IWAC components and projects the information onto a combining glass in front of the pilot. The data projected onto the combining glass includes navigational information and aiming symbols for weapon delivery. Primary controls for the HUD are on the HUD control panel. Additional controls are provided on the reversionary sight/nose camera control panel.

4. The missile system consists of two AIM-9 Sidewinder missiles that may be carried on the outboard pylons to provide an additional air-to-air attack capability. Operating controls and indicators for the AIM-9 missiles are on the Sidewinder control panel, the left glare shield, and the control stick. Aiming symbols for missile firing are presented to the pilot on the HUD combining glass.

MISCELLANY:

1. There is an optically flat glass panel on the port side of the nose accommodating an F.95 oblique camera. There is also a cockpit voice recorder to compliment the oblique camera.

2. The air refueling probe acts as a lift surface on the left side of the aircraft during flight and is unbalanced by lack of a similar surface on the right side. At intermediate angles of attack

the effect of the probe is negligible. However, as angle of attack increases or decreases from the intermediate range, the probe assumes undesirable flight characteristics. At increasing angles of attack, the probe will cause a yaw and roll to the right. At angles of attack below the intermediate range, the probe causes a yaw and roll to the left. In either case, when an extreme angle of attack is reached, the probe can

In a shallow dive toward its target, an AV-8A (BuNo. 158961) releases its two 500 pounders. AV-8A has impressive external stores capability and in many respects is equal or superior to the capabilities of the highly touted Douglas A-4. *McDonnell Douglas photo by Harry Gann*

VMA-231 AV-8A (BuNo. 158390) cruises serenely off California coast following gunnery exercise. *British Aerospace photo 741471*

Four 500 lb. Mk. 82 Snakeye bombs drop away from an AV-8A during training exercises at Yuma MCAS, Arizona. *McDonnell Douglas photo HG 77-374C by Harry Gann*

Harriers of VMA-513 on the prowl - each loaded with 5-inch FFAR Zuni rockets and napalm. Note that only the lower two aircraft carry the Aden gun pods. *Hawker Siddeley photo 723098 via Isham.*

cause a snap-departure from controlled flight.

ACCIDENT RECORD: A 1982 report showed that the Marines had lost 42 Harriers to various causes in the last eleven years. Of the original 110 AV-8s (including 8 TAV-8A's), only 68 were in service as of this writing. A consequence of these loses is the reduction of squadron strength from 20 to 15. Approximately half of these accidents were attributed to pilot error . . . and half of those occured during conventional flight. TAV-8A syllabus flight hours have increased from 16.8 hours of 64.3 total hours to 31 hours of 68.4 total hours. The chart (at right) compares the AV-8's accident record to that of other Navy aircraft.

The Harrier routinely performs its mission in shorter time (less flight hours per sortie) than conventional jet aircraft, and from unconventional air base facilities, thus exposing it to the increased hazards of takeoffs and landings more times during a given number of hours. Since flight hours are used in the measurement base, this tends to skew the rate in favor of conventional aircraft.

AV-8A PROGRAM COSTS: The 102 AV-8A's and 8 TAV-8A's were procured for $474.4 million. The average cost per airplane was $4.3 million.

AV-8B PROGRAM COSTS: Through FY-80 $446 million has been approved for Research and Development. As of August 1980, $379 million has been obligated. Both the House and Senate Armed Services Committee authorized $243 million of R & D and $90 million of procurement in FY-81. Long term plans call for the acquisitions 336 aircraft at a total cost of $8.2 billion.

AIRCRAFT	YEARS	NO. ACCIDENTS	HRS	ACCIDENT RATE
AV-8	71-80	42	113,738	3.69
F-8	57-66	743	1,473,491	5.04
A-4	57-66	668	2,515,026	2.66
F-4	61-70	378	1,267,050	2.98

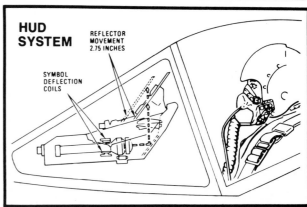

HUD SYSTEM

REFLECTOR MOVEMENT 2.75 INCHES

SYMBOL DEFLECTION COILS

AV-8A WEAPON POSSIBILITIES

NAME	DESCRIPTION	WEIGHT (LB)
Mk-76	Practice Bomb	24
Mk-77	Fire Bomb	520
Mk-81*	Low Drag General Purpose Bomb	270
Mk-82*	Low Drag General Purpose Bomb	530
Mk-82 LGB	Laser Guided General Purpose Bomb	601-617
Mk-83	Low Drag General Purpose Bomb	985
Mk-83 LGB	Laser Guided General Purpose Bomb	1098
Mk-86	Practice Bomb	200
Mk-87	Practice Bomb	330
Mk-88	Practice Bomb	794
Mk-106	Practice Bomb	5
Mk-124	Snakeye Practice Bomb	565
AN/ALE-37	Dispenser	186**
LAU-10	Four Tube Rocket Launcher	105**
LAU-60/61/69	Nineteen Tube Rocket Launcher	79/133/98**
LAU-68	Seven Tube Rocket Launcher	67**
SUU-40/44	Flare and Sensor Dispenser	132**
2.75 in FFAR	Folding Fin Aircraft Rocket	17-28
5.0 in FFAR	Folding Fin Aircraft Rocket	109-132
AN/SSQ-23 to 53	Sonobuoy	18-39
Mk-45	Paraflare	28
CBU-59	Antipersonnel and Antimateriel Weapon	760
CBU-72	Fuel Air Explosive Weapon	521
Mk-20	Rockeye Antitank Cluster Bomb	490
AIM-9G/H	Sidewinder Antiaircraft Missile	197
Gun Pod	ADEN 30mm Machine Gun	323**

* Also Available in Snakeye Retarded Versions   **Empty Weight

Loading 250 pound Mk 81, Snakeye bomb onto AV-8A wing pylon. Photo taking during Atlantic Ocean cruise on board *USS Guadalcanal* (LPH-7). *U.S. Navy photo K-89299 by Wade Davis*

Harrier pilot models standard flight suit for AV-8 operations. External garment is g-suit. Note heavy emphasis on survival gear. *Aerophile photo*

Marine Corps pilots depart from their AV-8A's following Mediterranean Sea sortie while on board carrier USS Franklin D. Roosevelt (CV-42). U.S. Navy photo 1168923 by Greg Haas

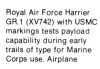

Royal Air Force Harrier GR.1 (XV742) with USMC markings tests payload capability during early trials of type for Marine Corps use. Airplane mounts five 250 pounders and two cluster bombs as well as usual ADEN cannon armament. Rolls Royce photo E223812

Unusual bicycle undercarriage of Harrier is rugged, lightweight, and small. Both main and nose gear retract into fuselage wells. Nose gear is steerable. ADEN cannon pods are mounted on airplane in photo. Aerophile photo

Fuselage ventral strakes are mounted in the place of the ADEN gun pods when the latter are not in place. Strakes improve hovering efficiency of AV-8 by trapping reflected exhaust efflux under fuselage. Note retractable cockpit entrance/egress step to right of photo. Aerophile photo

VMA-231 AV-8A shown during Mediterranean Sea exercises on board the carrier USS Franklin D. Roosevelt (CV-42). Note multiple ejector racks. U.S. Navy photo 1168914 by Greg Haas

THE TAV-8A

The TAV-8A is a two-place operational trainer aircraft logically and economically developed from the AV-8A. TAV-8As were procured for the Marine Corps and delivery to the AV-8A training squadron, VMAT-203, started in 1975.

TAV-8A PHYSICAL CHARACTERISTICS: The engine, wing, center fuselage, horizontal tail, rudder and landing gear are common to the AV-8A and TAV-8A. To accommodate the second crew member, the cockpit of the AV-8A has been moved forward 47 inches and an additional cockpit inserted behind and above the forward cockpit. The vertical tail of the TAV-8A has more area and greater height than does the vertical tail of the AV-8A. A TAV-8A with one crew member weighs approximately 850 pounds more than an AV-8A with a similar fuel and armament load.

When two crew members fly a TAV-8A it weighs approximately 1300 pounds more than an AV-8A in a similar configuration. When flying solo the pilot of the TAV-8A flies from the forward cockpit, but when two crew members man the same aircraft the pilot-in-command occupies the rear cockpit. Cockpits have dual flight controls and instruments with the principal switches and controls in the rear cockpit overriding those in the front cockpit. All operational features can be demonstrated from either cockpit. Each is equipped with a fully automatic ejection seat which provides safe escape to zero altitude and speed, even at high sink rates at low altitude.

TAV-8A PERFORMANCE CHARACTERISTICS: The TAV-8A permits conversion training in V/STOL techniques and proficiency training and testing in the use of navigation and attack systems. It is designed to the full AV-8A combat maneuvering envelope by local strengthening of areas otherwise unchanged. Handling qualities of the TAV-8A in wingborne flight are similar to those of the AV-8A. V/STOL handling characteristics are only slightly different from those of the AV-8A despite the increase in pitching inertia. All phases of light including weapon aiming technique and delivery accuracy can be monitored by the instructor via his Head Up Display in the rear cockpit. Visibility has been improved since the front cockpit is farther forward and the rear cockpit is higher than the AV-8A cockpit. The TAV-8A is also an excellent platform for teaching thrust vectoring techniques in air combat.

Canopy explosive cord is readily discernible in this photo of a VMAT-203 TAV-8A front canopy. Cord explodes just as ejection handles are pulled, thus allowing clean penetration for seat and crewmember. *L.M. Ricker photo*

Three quarter rear view of VMAT-203 TAV-8B (BuNo. 159383), taken in 1979, illustrates several important differences between this model and single-seat AV-8A. Note greatly extended tail cone for improved moment-arm action of rear yaw puffer. Also note extended height of vertical fin and ventral fin of different configuration. *L.M. Ricker photo*

This exceptional photo shows a TAV-8A of VMAT-203, ready for flight, at Quantico MCAF, Virginia. *U.S. Marine Corps photo A569098 by J.A. Harris*

Additional detail of TAV-8B canopy configuration shows close-up of rear windscreen and rear canopy in closed position. Strip under 05 i.d. number is night formation flying light. Strip glows pale green during night formation work and permits other aircraft crew members to see airplane for safe formation flying. *L.M. Ricker photo*

AV-8A on the left sits statically while TAV-8A (BuNo. 159382) of VMAT-203 on right is given a final groundcrew check before taxiing out for training mission. Note TAV-8A's extended canopy and elongated cockpit section. *L.M. Ricker photo*

Two VMAT-203 TAV-8A's on ramp at NAS Cherry Point. Side-opening canopy details unique to this model are apparent, as are slightly different camouflage details. *Rolls Royce photo*

Elongated cockpit of TAV-8A is readily apparent in this photo. Airplane weight is nearly a thousand pounds more than that of standard single-seat AV-8A. Note relocation of strike camera under second crew station. Also note explosive canopy cord just visible over crewmembers. *L.M. Ricker photo*

Another view of TAV-8A (BuNo. 159383) empennage. Lengthened tail cone to improve moment-arm effectivity of rear puffer is quite apparent, as is increased height of vertical fin. *L.M. Ricker photo*

VMAT-203 TAV-8A sits statically on Cherry Point ramp. Side-hinged canopy is a significant change from AV-8A's rearward-sliding type. *Cherry Point MCAS photo 0082-01-76*

LEFT

TAV·8A

SCALE VIEWS (1/72)

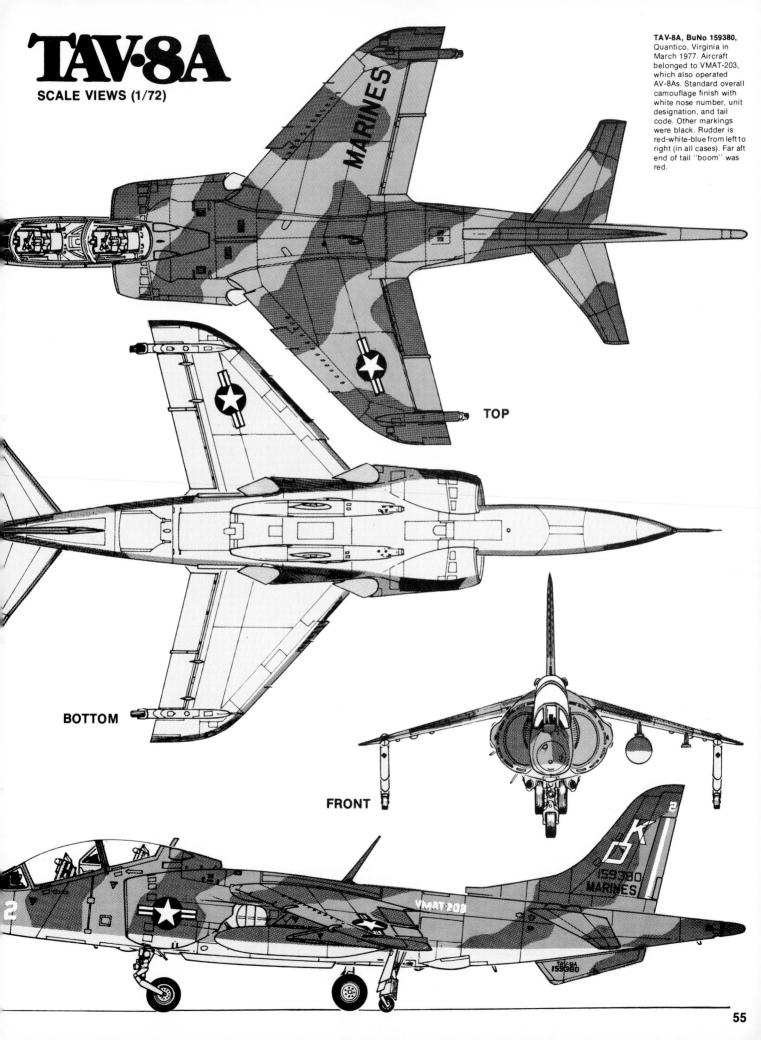

TAV-8A, BuNo 159380, Quantico, Virginia in March 1977. Aircraft belonged to VMAT-203, which also operated AV-8As. Standard overall camouflage finish with white nose number, unit designation, and tail code. Other markings were black. Rudder is red-white-blue from left to right (in all cases). Far aft end of tail "boom" was red.

TOP

BOTTOM

FRONT

OTHER AV-8 VARIANTS
THE AV-8B

On May 19, 1973, the Commandant of the Marine Corps, General R.E. Cushman, signed a letter to the CNO recommending a Specific Operating Requirement (SOR) for an advanced vectored thrust V/STOL light attack aircraft. The SOR included a specific statement of the requirements for an all V/STOL light attack force. This requirement was reiterated by General Cushman on February 19, 1974 when he told the Senate Armed Services Committee that:

"The operational success of the AV-8A program has confirmed our belief that V/STOL technology is sound and that a follow-on aircraft will meet our needs for future light attack requirements and permit us to achieve our goal of an all V/STOL light attack force."

This led to the AV-8B Advanced Harrier V/STOL program, which was formalized at DSARC I in March 1976. The program consists of four parts:
- A six month period of Contract Definition.
- A two aircraft YAV-8B flight demonstration program.
- A four aircraft full scale development program.
- A production program of approximately 350 aircraft for the Marine Corps.

The current estimated cost of the full scale development program is substantially less than that needed to develop a new conventional aircraft of the AV-8B's size.

AV-8B PERFORMANCE: In the past it has been necessary to give up some payload-radius performance in order to have V/STOL. This was true with the AV-8A, but to acquire the flexibility of vertical and short takeoff and landing the Marines were willing to trade performance for effectiveness. The AV-8B is a different situation. For example:
- Without increasing engine thrust, the AV-8B doubles (from a vertical takeoff) or triples (from a short takeoff) the payload-radius capability of the AV-8A.
- With six Mk-82 500-lb bombs, the AV-8B has a radius 55% greater than the A-4M Skyhawk. For this mission the AV-8B uses only 1250 ft for takeoff compared to the A-4M's 4200 ft.
- With a 5100 lb payload, the AV-8B (900 ft. short takeoff) has a radius equal to that of the A-7 (5600 ft of ground roll).
- The AV-8B has a maximum ordnance payload capability of 9200 pounds.

All of this is achieved while realizing the basing flexibility and quick reaction which V/STOL provides. Vertical takeoff from small pads or platform ships, short takeoff for maximum payload or radius, operations from bombed runways, and the use of thrust vectoring for in-flight maneuvering make the AV-8B a highly effective and survivable weapon system. The AV-8B has performance as good as or better than a cross-section of current attack aircraft. Rather than a penalty, V/STOL in the AV-8B is an added benefit.

AV-8B TECHNOLOGY: To achieve its performance advantages the AV-8B incorporates state-of-the-art advanced technology. Major elements are:
- New wing aerodynamics from the supercritical airfoil shape. This is the first application in military attack aircraft of this NASA-developed technology. Drag is reduced, lift is increased, and the thicker cross-section accommodates more fuel than conventional designs.
- Advanced structural material (graphite epoxy) is used instead of metals in most of the wing (63% by weight). The AV-8B wing is the first of this kind of any aircraft in the world. This new material saves 300 pounds, has unusually long life, and does not corrode.
- A new single slotted flap is integrated with the Pegasus engine exhaust nozzles. The result of this aero-propulsion combination is over 6700 pounds of added short takeoff lift (compared to the AV-8A).
- Simple, lightweight fences under the fuselage increase vertical takeoff capability by 1200 pounds compared to

TAV-8A REAR COCKPIT

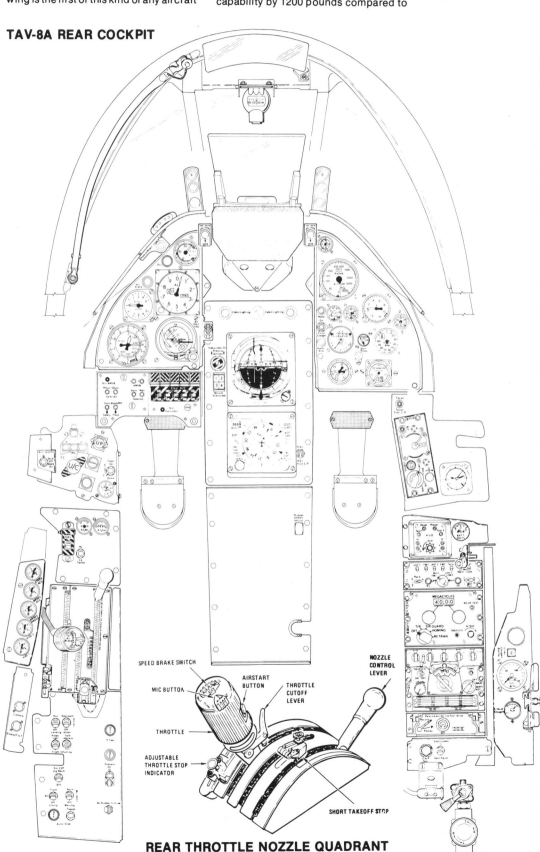

REAR THROTTLE NOZZLE QUADRANT

the AV-8A.

• A redesigned air inlet system increases the useful thrust of the Pegasus engine by 600 pounds. And a new configuration of the two forward exhaust nozzles adds another 200 pounds of thrust.

• Incorporation of the latest in avionics, stores management, and other systems, improves effectiveness, reliability, and maintainability.

The most important technology involved is the design integration of all these items into a practical aircraft configuration. These technologies and the AV-8B have significance beyond the recognized USMC requirement for effective close air support. They impact the design of future aircraft, conventional and V/STOL, maintain U.S. leadership in aeronautics, V/STOL in particular, and provide the necessary performance to fully exploit V/STOL operational potential on land and sea.

This significance has been recognized by the Department of Defense and by Congress. In testimony before the Senate Armed Services Committee on 9 February 1978, Secretary of the Navy W. Graham Claytor stated:

"I think it is very important that V/STOL technology as represented by the AV-8B aircraft development program . . . be pursued not only for the Marine Corps close air support mission, but also for the contribution our continuing experience with V/STOL can make to future naval V/STOL development."

This position was reinforced by the House Appropriations Committee which states in its Report No. 95-1398:

"The AV-8B is the only viable V/STOL program in progress. It is helping to pave the way for the future by taking existing technology and improving upon it, and by fostering a climate in which more advanced V/STOL concepts could be pursued. In the Committee's view, the AV-8B technology could provide a logical transition to the Navy's Type B V/STOL aircraft planned for the late 1990s."

The Marine Corps has never waivered in its commitment to V/STOL aircraft, and for good reason. As Lt. Gen. Thomas Miller testified before the Senate Armed Services Committee in March 1978:

"The AV-8B will provide Marine ground forces with the most effective close air support available through the 1990s".

THE YAV-8B PROGRAM

The initial studies for the YAV-8B program were initiated in May 1975 under guidelines from NAVAIR Program Management (PMA-257). Its primary purposes are to advance V/STOL technology and verify AV-8B design and program objectives with a goal of AV-8B Initial Operating Capability (IOC) in 1984.

The YAV-8B effort comprises two phases. Phase I (1 April 1976 through 31 October 1976) assessed advanced technology previously developed in V/STOL studies, and developed a program plan for transitioning into Phase II. The AV-8B full scale wind tunnel program was completed on 18 September 1976 during which the AV-8B VTO and STO performance capabilities were demonstrated, the inlet characteristics documented, the high lift

configuration optimized, and the stability and control characteristics shown to be as good as or better than those of the AV-8A.

Phase II, the Flight Demonstration Phase of the YAV-8B program, is a 32-month effort for the period of 1 November 1976 through June 1979. The following major objectives of the YAV-8B program are being demonstrated in the flight demonstration program:

• Improved payload radius and takeoff performance.

• Improved reliability and maintainability.

• Increased external load capability (more store stations).

• Increased propulsion system efficiency through inlet and nozzle improvements.

• Satisfactory handling throughout the operational flight envelope.

• Flight experience on production relevant components and systems.

Major program elements consist of designing, manufacturing, and flight testing two YAV-8B aircraft. Manufacture of YAV-8B No. 1 was completed on 1 September 1978 and after systems checkout, first flight was successfully accomplished on 9 November 1978, 53 days ahead of schedule. The second YAV-8B flew for the first time on 19 February 1979.

The two YAV-8Bs were fabricated by modifying two AV-8As. These modifications incorporated AV-8B aerodynamic advancements including an improved inlet with a larger auxiliary inlet system for increased propulsive lift, LIDs for additional vertical lift, and a new larger, higher-aspect-ratio wing. The wing has a supercritical airfoil section and utilizes a positive circulation flap to achieve high lift when operating in the Rolling Vertical Takeoff (RVTO) and short-takeoff modes. The major wing

Cockpit detail of TAV-8A rear seat. Back seat cockpit is quite similar to front seat in accouterments. Note that it is even equipped with operational HUD. *L.M. Ricker* photo

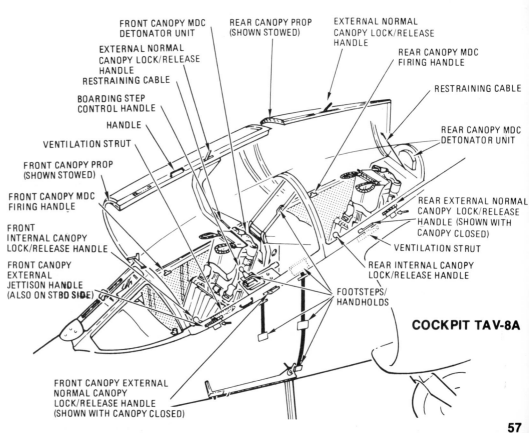

FRONT CANOPY MDC DETONATOR UNIT

REAR CANOPY PROP (SHOWN STOWED)

EXTERNAL NORMAL CANOPY LOCK/RELEASE HANDLE

EXTERNAL NORMAL CANOPY LOCK/RELEASE HANDLE RESTRAINING CABLE

REAR CANOPY MDC FIRING HANDLE

BOARDING STEP CONTROL HANDLE

RESTRAINING CABLE

HANDLE

REAR CANOPY MDC DETONATOR UNIT

VENTILATION STRUT

FRONT CANOPY PROP (SHOWN STOWED)

FRONT CANOPY MDC FIRING HANDLE

REAR EXTERNAL NORMAL CANOPY LOCK/RELEASE HANDLE (SHOWN WITH CANOPY CLOSED)

FRONT INTERNAL CANOPY LOCK/RELEASE HANDLE

VENTILATION STRUT

FRONT CANOPY EXTERNAL JETTISON HANDLE (ALSO ON STBD SIDE)

REAR INTERNAL CANOPY LOCK/RELEASE HANDLE

FOOTSTEPS/ HANDHOLDS

COCKPIT TAV-8A

FRONT CANOPY EXTERNAL NORMAL CANOPY LOCK/RELEASE HANDLE (SHOWN WITH CANOPY CLOSED)

The supercritical graphite-epoxy wing is very evident in this construction view of the YAV-8B. *McDonnell Douglas photo C12-6572-22*

AV-8B mock-up undergoes full-scale wind tunnel tests at NASA's Ames Research Center, just outside San Francisco, California. Tests, conducted before first actual flight of AV-8B, were undertaken inside NASA's 40x80 foot tunnel — which is the largest in the world. *NASA photo 76-H-742*

The Pegasus engine is shown here illustrating its size relative to the YAV-8B. *Rolls Royce photo*

First flight of the YAV-8B (BuNo 158394). *McDonnell Douglas photo C12-7176-96*

Sea trials of YAV-8B No. 1 aboard the *U.S.S. Saipan* occurring in October of 1979, proved quite successful. Note AV-8B's repositioned balancing wheels. *McDonnell Douglas photo C12-8463-583*

Many of the special features of the YAV-8B are in evidence here including redesigned forward nozzles, double supplementary air doors, and revised hard points and outrigger gear positions. *McDonnell Douglas photo C12-8463-161*

structural elements are of composite materials. The YAV-8B engine is a F402 Pegasus II series including a new gear box and forward nozzles. These changes provide more than twice the mission performance of the AV-8A.

The YAV-8B also incorporates selective system modifications which improve reliability and maintainability, thus permitting a brief flight demonstration program to validate the improved mission availability of the AV-8B.

In addition to the flight demonstration, technical trade studies are keeping abreast of latest technological advances and how they can further enhance the technology of the AV-8B. In particular, improvements in reliability and maintainability, aircraft performance, survivability and vulnerability, service life, and acquisition, operational, and maintenance costs are being fully explored. Contract data is being developed and submitted to permit an orderly transition into Full Scale Development.

All the technical elements incorporated into the YAV-8B configuration have been either tested (LIDS), wind tunnel tested (STO lift improvement), or laboratory tested (composites).

A summary to date of YAV-8B flight demonstration accomplishments is shown below. These flights have demonstrated excellent handling qualities in all test areas. For vertical takeoffs and landings the aircraft is more stable in ground effect than the AV-8A, while pilot workload is reduced by 65 percent. Vertical landing in 25 kt winds, gusting to 35 kt. is comfortable. In hover, maneuvering is smooth, positive and precise; height capture is easy and precise, and the aircraft is very stable in roll. Handling qualities in semijetborne flight are comfortable, lateral control is quick and positive. In wingborne flight to 470 KIAS handling qualities are excellent with good lateral control, good longitudinal damping following stick raps, and comfortable 360 degree rolls. Slow approach and short landing modes are comfortable with low workload, hardly noticeable ground effect on longitudinal trim, and good control on runway after touchdown.

FLIGHT DEMONSTRATION HIGHLIGHTS (JULY 1980)

- Flights — 226
- Flight Hours — 246.3 Hours
- Takeoff Weight
  — VTO (47.5°F) — 19,972 lb
  — STO (588 ft. Roll) — 28,084 lb
- Flight Duration (Internal Fuel) — 2.1 hrs
- Airspeed — 0 to 500 Knots
- Altitude — Sea Level to 45,400 ft.
- Normal Load Factor — -1.6 to 7 "g"
- 20 Test Flights — 6 Days
- Maximum Mach — 0.96
- Pilot Workload — Reduced 65%
- NPE and OPEVAL Complete

AV-8B TECHNOLOGY HIGHLIGHTS

Supercritical Airfoil
- More lift for maneuvering
- More efficient cruise
- More internal fuel

Positive Circulation
- More STO lift

Composite Structures
- Saves Weight
- More Payload
- Longer Life

Fiber Optics
- EMI/EMP Immunity
- Greater Bandwidth

Lift Improvement Devices
- More VTO Lift
- Reduced Inlet Ingestion

Improved Inlet
- More VTO Lift
- Better Cruise Efficiency

Zero Scarf Nozzles
- Increased Thrust

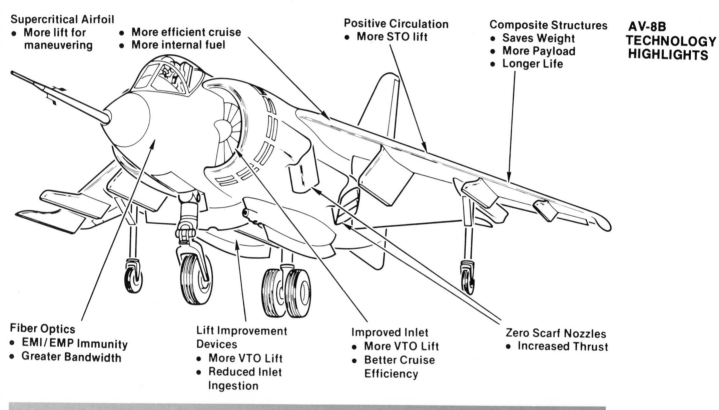

Second AV-8B (BuNo. 158395) prototype is shown in flight with full weapons compliment in place. Besides two AIM-9L's, airplane is also carrying seven 250-pound retarded free-fall bombs, and its normal compliment of cannon. Note retracted balancing wheels. *McDonnell Douglas photo C22-133-1*

Prototype AV-8B's are extensively modified AV-8A's incorporating new wing, new intakes, and many other changes. Production AV-8B's will be considerably different and will have new forward fuselage section as well as other modifications. *McDonnell Douglas photo*

SCALE VIEWS (1/72)

YAV·8B

YAV-8B, BuNo 158394, St. Louis, Missouri, early 1979. Number one AV-8B prototype was glossy white overall with insignia red and medium blue. Anti-glare panel was flat black. Side flash, tail and elevon bands, and wing tips were red. Spine, pitot, canopy frame, wing tip and tail band piping in medium blue. "MARINES", tail number and Bureau Number in black. "AV-8B", gear and wheels are white. Nozzles were dark natural metal.

OUTRIGGER LANDING GEAR

MARINES

TOP

MCDONNELL DOUGLAS

Detail illustrates early lettering carried on first flight of YAV-8B.

AV·8B

MARINES

158

AV·8B

LEFT

AV-8B DESCRIPTION

The dramatic improvements in performance capabilities of the AV-8B over those of the AV-8A are a result of state-of-the-art development in several technological areas including aerodynamics, propulsion, composite structures and avionics. Technological highlights include a composite wing with supercritical airfoil and positive circulation flaps, improved inlet, lift improvement devices, enlarged composite forward fuselage with raised cockpit, modern avionics with an Angle Rate Bombing System (ARBS) for weapons delivery and a Stabilization Augmentation and Attitude Hold System (SAAHS), which provides stability augmentation for pitch, roll, and yaw control in hover and transition. Combined with small engine improvements, these advances increase mission capability and pilot visibility while reducing workload and improving handling qualities. Landing minimums are reduced and flight safety is increased by incorporation of an all-weather

Three views of the final McDonnell Douglas-built full-scale mock-up of the production-configured AV-8B as it appeared in August 1975. This was released prior to the roll-out and first flights of the two prototype YAV-8B's. Aircraft in mock-up form differs somewhat from YAV-8B configuration in that balancing wheels are of a slightly different configuration and wing pylons are of a slightly larger size. AV-8B intake configuration, as tested on YAV-8B's is also somewhat different than that shown on mock-up. *McDonnell Douglas photos*

landing system. Reliability and maintainability improvements providing greater optional readiness complement these changes.

In addition to technological advances, significant configuration improvements have been incorporated including increased fuel capacity, improved hydraulic system, increased armament capability, improved reaction controls, and R&M improvements.

PROPULSION SYSTEM: The F402 series Pegasus propulsion system has been service proven by the 350 units already built. This engine has undergone continuous improvement, and the ongoing Product Support Program (PSP) continues to provide candidate improvements through component and engine tests. The AV-8B propulsion system, designated the F402-RR-404, consists of a derivative of the F402 series and the improved inlet developed on the YAV-8B program. The F402-RR-404 engine provides increased engine life and a significant improvement in reliability and maintainability over the F402-RR-402. The major modifications incorporated in the F402-RR-404 include an uprated gear box, new bulkhead for the AV-8B wing line, and zero-scarf

nozzles. The AV-8B inlet provides increased total pressure recovery in V/STOL conditions and reduced pressure distortion during conventional flight. The thrust is increased by 250 lb.

WEIGHT COMPARISON: Extensive use of composite materials, representing over 23% of the structure, and state-of-the-art advancements in systems design have resulted in the improved capabilities of the AV-8B while maintaining excellent balance and a small increase in operating weight empty from the AV-8A. A weight comparison is shown below. As can be seen from this comparison, maximum takeoff gross weight and hence payload has increased significantly due to both increased thrust and aerodynamic improvements.

WEAPON CAPABILITIES: The AV-8B weapon carrying capabilities have been expanded to seven stations (three on each wing and one on the fuselage centerline) as compared to five stations for the AV-8A. These seven stations offer four wet stations, four air-to-air missile stations, four air-to-ground missile stations, two nuclear stations, and five Triple Ejector Rack (TER) stations.

ENGINE RATING COMPARISON

	THRUST (LB)	
RATING	*AV-8A*	*AV-8B*
Short Lift Wet	20,930	21,180
Short Lift Dry	19,920	20,120
Normal Lift Wet	20,395	20,600
Normal Lift Dry	19,020	19,230
Maximum Thrust	16,350	16,530
Maximum Continuous	13,100	13,240
Idle	1,000	1,000

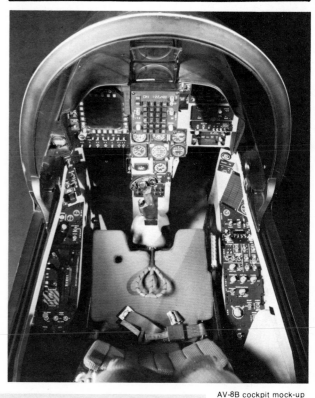

AV-8A AND AV-8B WEIGHT COMPARISON

	WEIGHT (LB)		
	AV-8A*	*WEIGHT CHANGE*	*AV-8B*
Weight Empty	11,890	583	12,473
Operating Weight Empty	12,191	559	12,750
Basic Flight Design Gross Weight	20,600	2,352	22,952
Maximum Takeoff Gross Weight			
STO	24,600	5,150	29,750
VTO	17,050	2,135	19,185

*Based on aircraft no. 108

AV-8B cockpit mock-up photo shows advanced technology incorporated in its design. Cockpit is simpler, less cluttered, and significantly more modular in concept than earlier AV-8A. *McDonnell Douglas photo C12-8334-11*

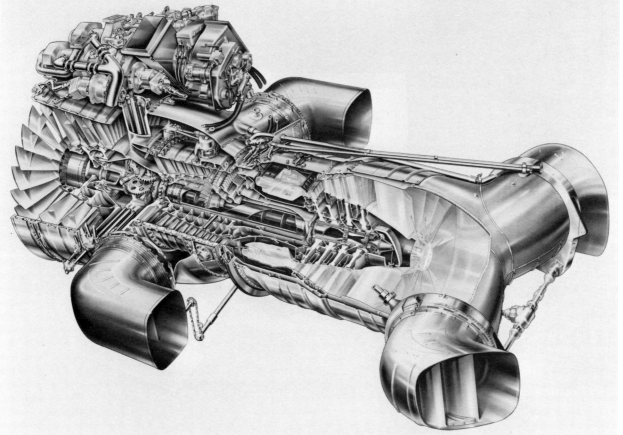

Detailed cutaway of Rolls Royce Pegasus engine illustrates type's unique articulated exhaust nozzles and hot and cold thrust systems. Fan section air, which is relatively cool, exhausts out the forward set of nozzles, and burner section gases, which are extremely hot, exhaust out the rear set. Engine version illustrated in drawing has AV-8B-type nozzles. *Rolls Royce photo E221027*

AV-8A AND AV-8B ARMAMENT CAPABILITY

STORES	TOTAL PER AIRCRAFT	
	AV-8A	*AV-8B*
Missiles		
AIM-9H/L Sidewinder	4	4
AGM-65/E Laser Guided Maverick	-	4
General Purpose Bombs		
Mk-81 LDGP Conical Fin	5	16
Mk-81 Snakeye	5	16
Mk-82 LDGP Conical Fin	5	16
Mk-82 Snakeye	5	16
Mk-83 LDGP Conical Fin	2	6
Destructors		
Mk-36 Mods 1a,2,3,4 (Mk-82 Body) Conical Fin	5	16
Mk-36 Mods 1a, 2, 3, 4 (Mk-82 Body) S.E. High Drag/Low Drag	5	16
Mk-40 Mods 1a,2,3,4 (Mk-83 Body) Concial Fin	2	6
Mk-40 Mods 1a,2,3,4 (Mk-83 Body) S.E. High Drag/Low Drag	2	6
Laser Guided Bombs		
Mk-82 LGB GBU-12B/B	4	10
Mk-83 LGB GBU-16/B	2	4
Cluster Bombs		
APAM CBU-59/B	3	8
CBU-72/B FAEI	5	10
BLU-95/B FAE II	-	10
Rockeye II Mods 2/3/4/6	5	12
Fire Bombs		
Mk-77 (Mod 2/4)	5	10
Rocket Launchers		
LAU-10A/A,B/A,C/A,D/A	4	10
LAU-61 A/A	4	10
LAU-68 B/A	4	10
Dispensers		
SUU-44/A (Mk-24/45 Flares)	2	6
SUU-44/A (SSQ-23A Sono Buoys)	2	6
SUU-44/A (SSQ-50 Sono Buoys)	2	6
Special Weapons		
D-57 (Wiring Only)	-	2
B-61 (Wiring Only)	-	2
Miscellaneous Stores		
CNU-183/A EBC	2	2
Airborne Self-Protection Jam Pod	-	1
GPU-2/A (M-197) Gun Pod	-	2
Suspension Hardware		
14 in./30 in. Pylon Extension Unit	-	2
ADU-299A/A Adapter (Sidewinder)	2	2
LAU-7A-4 Launcher (Sidewinder)	2	4
LAU-117A Launcher (Maverick)	-	4
Centerline Pylon	1	1
Inboard Pylon	2	2
Intermediate Pylon	-	2
Outboard Pylon	2	2

SUPERCRITICAL WING: The AV-8B new supercritical airfoil with positive circulation flap, developed on the YAV-8B program, has 15% more area than the AV-8A wing. The AV-8B wing is composed of a main torque box, trailing edge flap, aileron, and outrigger gear fairing all fabricated of advanced composite material, and a metal leading edge. The inboard portion of the main torque box is sealed and serves as an integral fuel tank. The wings are configured to accept six pylons. Inboard and intermediate stations contain external fuel provisions. A Reaction Control System (RCS) duct extends through the wing leading edges to valves located in the wing tips.

AVIONICS SYSTEM: The AV-8B avionics system provides improvements over the AV-8A system by utilizing existing state-of-the-art equipment integrated to provide a highly reliable and flexible system with extensive operational capability. The air-to-ground capability is acquired from the dual mode tracker (TV and laser) Angle Rate Bombing System (ARBS), which provides passive flexible, accurate weapon delivery. Navigation is provided by the ASN-130 Inertial Navigation System (INS), by TACAN or by air data. Pilot workload is reduced by using multipurpose controls and displays. In addition, air-to-air self-protection capability is provided by two Sidewinders and one 25mm gun. Survivability is further enhanced by radar warning, decoy dispensing systems and provisions for the Airborne Self-Protection Jammer pod.

Modern controls and displays have been carefully chosen to reduce pilot workload and optimize the use of panel area. The Hands On Throttle and Stick (HOTAS) control and the allocation of

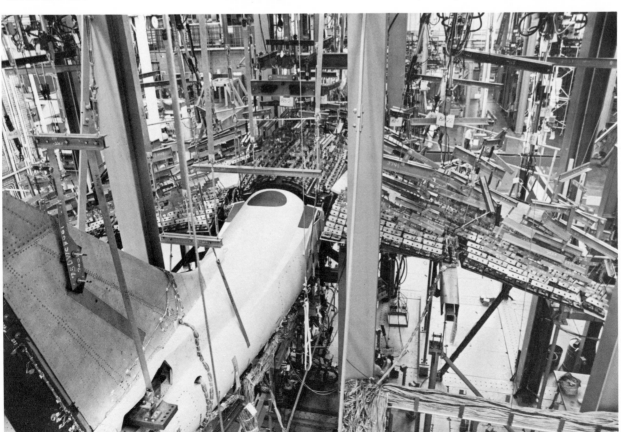

Beneath this jungle of bracing, straps, and tension pads is an AV-8B undergoing strain and stress testing by McDonnell Douglas engineers. Even under sixty tons of force, no damage to the airframe was sustained. *McDonnell Douglas photo 82-48*

housekeeping and nonpilot-decision tasks to the mission computer permit the pilot to concentrate on combat tasks. Inclusion of Stability Augmentation, Attitude Hold System (SAAHS) further reduces the workload while increasing safety.

The ARBS and Stores Management Set (SMS) provide accurate automatic and Continuously Computed Impact Point (CCIP) weapon delivery modes for clear day/night attack. Backup barometric weapon delivery modes and depressed sightline ensure that the AV-8B can deliver its weapons even if the primary weapon delivery system should fail.

The CNI complement of the AV-8B benefits from recent GFE developments. Two wideband (UHF/VHF) ARC-182

radios are used which, with the backup control panel, ensure communication capability at all times. The lightweight ARN-118 TACAN and the ARN-128 All-Weather Landing System are also recent GFE developments incorporated in the system.

The GFE, AYK-14 Mission Computer and its Operational Flight Program (OFP) have executive control of the avionics system. System interconnect is accomplished by dual, fully redundant, Type 1553A Multiplex Data Bus (MDB) systems. Message traffic on the MDB is controlled by the computer. A backup bus controller controls essential data should the mission computer fail.

Avionics installation is an intrinsic part of the weapon system design. It is especially important in the AV-8B which

has stringent weight and balance requirements. This installation is continuing to be refined to provide the best possible installation in terms of:
• Thermal/vibration/shock environment
• Maintainability
• Weight/balance
• Electromagnetic compatibility
These installation and environmental considerations will be used as the basis for design and testing of the avionic equipment.

PERFORMANCE CHARACTERISTICS:
The takeoff performance of the AV-8B is significantly improved over that of the AV-8A in both the VTO and STO modes. The increases in VTO performance stem from improved inlet recovery, the addition of the zero-scarf angle forward

AV-8B INBOARD PROFILE (NO SCALE)

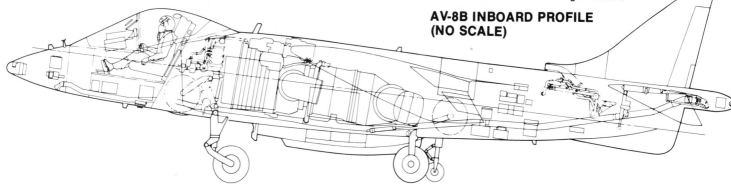

AV-8B CONFIGURATION CHANGES RELATIVE TO AV-8A

ITEM	CHANGE DESCRIPTION	COMMENT
INLET	THROAT AND HIGHLIGHT AREA ENLARGED	REDUCED DUCT VELOCITIES/HIGHER INLET RECOVERY
	DOUBLE DOOR AUXILIARY INLETS ADDED	INCREASED FLOW AREA/HIGHER RECOVERY
	ELLIPTICAL LIP SHAPE IN LIEU OF CIRCULAR	REDUCED DISTORTION
	EXTERNAL COWL RECONTOURED	REDUCED CRUISE DRAG/INCREASED FORWARD FUEL TANK CAPACITY
WING	NEW WING (230 SQ FT SUPERCRITICAL AIRFOIL WITH POSITIVE CIRCULATION FLAP)	IMPROVED LIFT/DRAG PERFORMANCE
	• WING/FUSELAGE INTERFACE REVISED	TO ACCOMMODATE IMPROVED WING
	• 6 PYLON STATIONS (4 WET)	INCREASED PAYLOAD
	• COMPOSITE MATERIALS	WEIGHT SAVINGS
	• FUEL CAPACITY INCREASED	INCREASED PAYLOAD RADIUS
LIFT IMPROVEMENT DEVICES (LIDS)	RETRACTABLE FUSELAGE ADDED	IMPROVED VTO LIFTOFF CAPABILITY
	FIXED LONGITUDINAL STRAKES ADDED	
AVIONICS AND ARMAMENT	ADDED:	
	• ANGLE RATE BOMBING (ARBS)	IMPROVED BOMBING ACCURACY
	• RADAR WARNING	INCREASED SURVIVABILITY
	• SECURE SPEECH	IMPROVED CLOSE AIR SUPPORT (CAS)
	• RADAR BEACON	IMPROVED CLOSE AIR SUPPORT (CAS)
	• LANDING AIDS (AWLS)	IMPROVED LANDING SAFETY
	• DECM POD PROVISIONS	IMPROVED SURVIVABILITY
	• ALE-39 CHAFF/FLARE PROVISIONS	IMPROVED SURVIVABILITY
	• MULTIPURPOSE DISPLAY	REDUCED PILOT WORKLOAD
	• ELECTRIC FUZING	MORE EFFECTIVE WEAPON DELIVERY
	• IMPROVED CNI	IMPROVED OPERATIONAL CAPABILITY
	• STORES MANAGEMENT SYSTEM	IMPROVED WEAPON DELIVERY
	• MAVERICK MISSILE	IMPROVED AIR-TO-GROUND CAPABILITY
	• WIRING PROVISIONS FOR SPECIAL STORES	GROWTH PROVISION
	• STABILITY AUGMENTATION ATTITUDE HOLD SYSTEM	IMPROVED FLYING QUALITIES - REDUCED PILOT WORKLOAD
	• INERTIAL NAVIGATION SYSTEM ASN-130	PRECISION NAVIGATION
	• IMPROVED AIR DATA COMPUTER	IMPROVED OPERATIONAL CAPABILITY
	• PRODUCTION RELEVANT DIGITAL TACAN	IMPROVED R&M AND WEIGHT REDUCTION
	• DIGITAL HSI	COMPATIBLE WITH TACAN
	REMOVED:	
	• ASN-116 AHRS	REPLACED BY ASN-130
OTHER	LANDING GEAR STRENGTHENED	TO MATCH INCREASED WEIGHT AND VERTICAL VELOCITY
	OUTRIGGERS MOVED INBOARD	INCREASED FLEXIBILITY OF OPERATION
	ALUMINUM MAIN AND NOSE GEAR WHEELS	INCREASED STRENGTH AND CORROSION RESISTANCE
	WHEELS AND TIRES STRENGTHENED	TO MATCH INCREASED WEIGHT AND VERTICAL VELOCITY
	AFT FUSELAGE STRUCTURE STRENGTHENED	DUE TO INCREASED TAIL LOADS AND INCREASED STRUCTURE LIFE

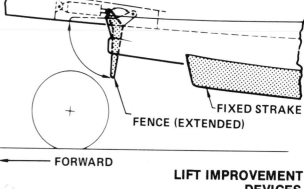

FIXED STRAKE

FENCE (EXTENDED)

FORWARD

LIFT IMPROVEMENT DEVICES

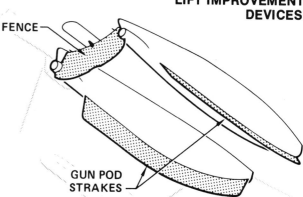

FENCE

GUN POD STRAKES

• ADVANCED ECM SYSTEMS
• SMOKELESS ENGINE
• MULTI-SPAR COMPOSITE WING
• INTEGRAL FUEL TANKS
• REDUNDANT ENGINE FUEL FEED
• CONTROL SYSTEM SPRING CARTRIDGES
• REACTION CONTROL SYSTEM
• REDUNDANT HYDRAULIC SYSTEMS
• LESS FLAMMABLE HYDRAULIC FLUID
• ELECTRICAL POWER NOT NEEDED FOR SAFE FLIGHT
• PODDED GUNS AND AMMUNITION
• ONBOARD OXYGEN GENERATING SYSTEM
• WHEELS-UP VERTICAL LANDING CAPABILITY

AV-8B SURVIVABILITY FEATURES

nozzles, and the use of LIDS. STO improvements result from the improved inlet recovery, and revised forward nozzles plus the semijetborne lift improvement generated by the positive circulation flap.

AV-8B payload-radius capability is effectively double that of the AV-8A in both VTO and STO modes. With its seven store stations, the AV-8B is capable of carrying up to 16 Mk-82 bombs, four 300 gallon external tanks, six Mk-83 bombs, four Maverick air-to-ground missiles, four AIM-9 air-to-air missiles, or ten LAU-10 rocket pods.

The VTO capability of the AV-8B is defined as 99% of the hover weight. The 1% thrust margin is included to achieve recommended acceleration from the ground and also to allow smooth transition to forward flight. This is based on December, 1974 flight tests of an AV-8A equipped with LIDs. Included in the 79 press-ups accomplished were 66 VTOs to hover out of ground effect in which successful VTOs up to hover weight were demonstrated. Additional flight tests have demonstrated that heavy weight VTOs can be followed by transition to wingborn flight even with Jet Pipe Temperature Limiter (JPTL) trimback occurring relatively early in the transition.

The nozzle rotation velocity and position are functions of STO weight and hover weight and represent a compromise between minimum ground roll distance and minimum distance to 50 feet. When the nozzles are rotated (at 90 deg./sec.), the flap nozzle interconnect drives the flaps (at 45.9 deg./sec.) to the maximum deflection position of 61.7°. The

Compared to the basic Harrier, the AV-8B is a much changed aircraft. Many of these changes are evident in this photo taken at rollout in October 1981. Of special note is the increased visibility from the raised cockpit, the extra wing-store stations, and the wing fences. *McDonnell Douglas photo C12-11222-92*

AV-8B
GENERAL ARRANGEMENT CUTAWAY

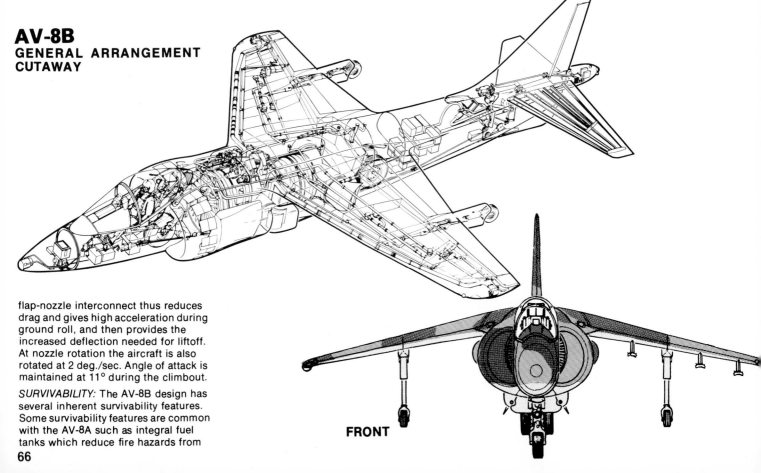

FRONT

flap-nozzle interconnect thus reduces drag and gives high acceleration during ground roll, and then provides the increased deflection needed for liftoff. At nozzle rotation the aircraft is also rotated at 2 deg./sec. Angle of attack is maintained at 11° during the climbout.

SURVIVABILITY: The AV-8B design has several inherent survivability features. Some survivability features are common with the AV-8A such as integral fuel tanks which reduce fire hazards from

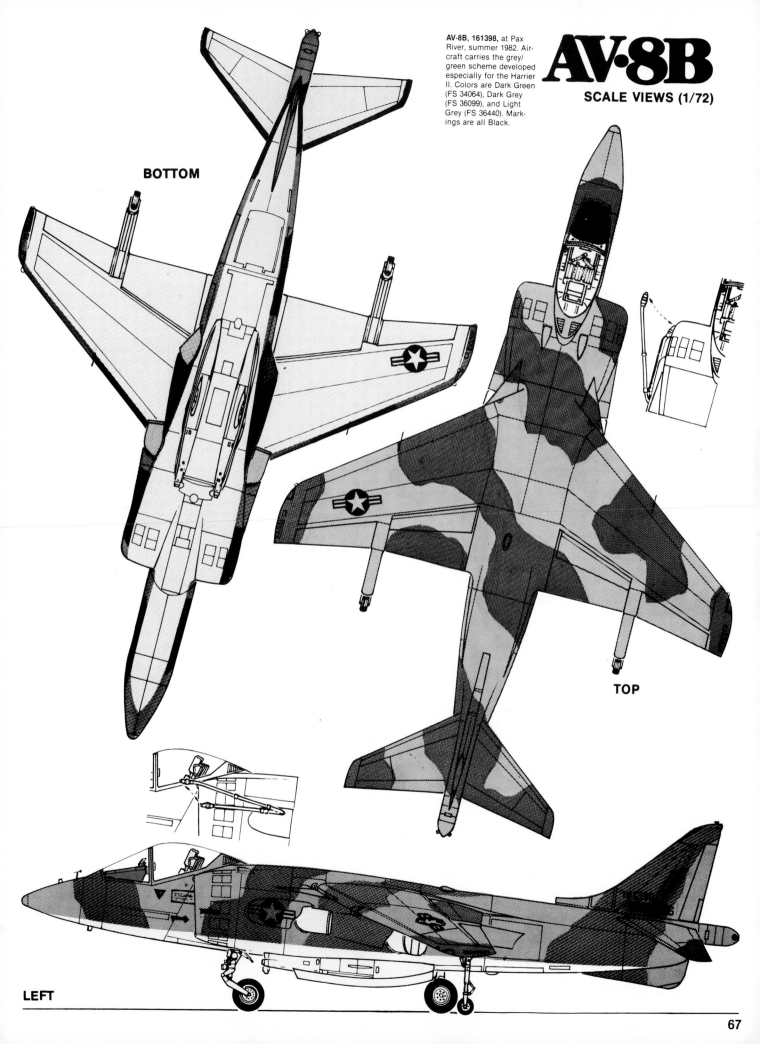

BOTTOM

AV-8B, 161398, at Pax River, summer 1982. Aircraft carries the grey/green scheme developed especially for the Harrier II. Colors are Dark Green (FS 34064), Dark Grey (FS 36099), and Light Grey (FS 36440). Markings are all Black.

AV·8B

SCALE VIEWS (1/72)

TOP

LEFT

internal fuel leakage, and the reaction control system which can serve as a partial backup in case of flight control surface damage.

Carrier takeoff capability is calculated using the techniques and assumptions described for STO calculations except that the nozzles are rotated approximately 50 feet from the end of the deck and the aircraft is rotated to 9° at the end of the deck. The aircraft climbs and accelerates using an angle of attack schedule.

Also, both the AV-8A and AV-8B feature flush mounted gun and ammunition pods which if hit tend to blow away from the aircraft with minimal structural damage to the basic airframe. Also both aircraft have redundant fuel and hydraulic systems allowing safe flight with only one system functional, and both aircraft have mechanical/fluid

power control systems such that electrical power is not needed for safe flight. Also the vertical landing capability is a survivability advantage since V/STOL aircraft can land softly if combat damage precludes landing gear extension. If the aircraft is otherwise damaged it can land vertically in an unplanned site to be airlifted to home base later.

Besides these basic features, the AV-8B design includes many features which improve survivability. AV-8B flight control survivability has been improved by use of the newer less flammable hydraulic fluid and installation of a spring cartridge which makes the aileron linkage inside the wing jam proof. The composite wing improves survivability because of greater damage tolerance than a corresponding metal wing. Also, the wing features multispar construction

which allows safe flight using multiple load paths if a major structural element is shot away. A third benefit is that composite skin is more resilient and therefore less prone to suffer hydraulic ram damage or produce flame holders or petaling if hits occur in the fueled portion of the wing. Also the AV-8B has an onboard oxygen generating system which provides pilot breathing capability without the necessity of liquid oxygen carried on the aircraft thereby reducing potential fire hazard.

The AV-8B also has features that reduce the enemy's ability to detect or hit it. Among these are smokeless engine, a reduced frontal IR signature due to additional pylon masking, and an advanced ECM system consisting of the ALR-67 radar warning receiver, the ALE-39 flare/chaff/minijammer dispenser, and a DECM pod jammer.

A Harrier II in hover tests at the McDonnell Douglas plant in St. Louis. This unusual shot of the lower surfaces reveals detail changes from the AV-8A . . . including inboard placement of wing-mounted alighting gear. *McDonnell Douglas photo C12-11328-92*

First full-scale AV-8B (161396) following October, 1981 rollout at McDonnell's St. Louis plant. Lift improvement devices are shown to good advantage. *McDonnell Douglas photo C12-11222-151*

Fatigue testing has shown that the Marines may expect as many as sixty years of rigorous flying out of the AV-8B. Its graphite-epoxy construction is credited with much of the success of the Harrier II during stress and strain tests equivalent to 24,000 actual flight hours.

Currently the Marine Corps requirement is for six developmental airframes and 336 production AV-8B's. Developmental airframes include four full-scale aircraft and two structural/fatigue test airframes.

The first flight of the AV-8B Advanced Harrier occured November 5, 1981 at the McDonnell Douglas plant with Charley Plummer at the controls. Originally scheduled for October, the flight was delayed when a foreign particle was ingested . . . requiring an engine change. The aircraft, BuNo 161396, is one of the four full-scale development aircraft built for flight testing. Three of these airframes will undergo tests at Patuxent River; the fourth will go to Edwards A.F.B. These four, along with the structural/fatigue test airframes will be followed by twelve pilot production AV-8B's in 1983. Operational testing will begin with the delivery of these 12 aircraft.

Under a collaborative agreement, Great Britain and the United States are sharing development and production of the Advanced Harrier. The Harrier II co-production agreement between McDonnell Douglas and British Aerospace provides for some 60 per cent of the work on U.S.M.C. and R.A.F. aircraft to be done by McDonnell Douglas, with British Aerospace picking up 40 per cent. Sales to third countries will be split 75% — McDonnell Douglas/25% — British Aerospace. The Pegasus engines will be built by Rolls-Royce, with the proviso that 25% of the value of the Marine Corps' engines be done by Pratt & Whitney. Anticipated production will include sixty of the aircraft for the Royal Air Force as GR.5's and 336 AV-8B's for the U.S. Marine Corps. Deliveries are to be spread out over a period of eight years.

Many observers feel that the Harrier II will be the first V/STOL aircraft in the world to justify real large scale production. Reasons cited include enhanced flight safety, high reliability, ease of servicing, and its increased combat loading/combat radius performance. The real significance of the AV-8B in the history of V/STOL development may be as an interim step between the AV-8A and a supersonic V/STOL fighter.

TAV-8B DESCRIPTION

NAVAIR is currently investigating the program option for meeting the USMC requirement for a two-seat V/STOL trainer. Procurement of TAV-8As or development and procurement of a TAV-8B design are the major options.

It should be emphasized, however, that the current plan (August 1980) is not to procure TAV-8B's, but instead, to procure TAV-8A's with updated capabilities. From a historical standpoint it was felt that information concerning the proposed TAV-8B program should be documented; thus it is included in this monograph.

The TAV-8B is a two-seat training and operational version of the AV-8B. It fulfills the USMC need for an AV-8B trainer while retaining the tactical combat capability of the AV-8B. The forward cockpit is identical to the AV-8B providing completely relevant V/STOL flight conversion training. The aft cockpit is equipped to allow the instructor pilot to monitor the performance of the student pilot and provides take-command and get-home capabilities, if required. The aft cockpit may also be used by student pilots for navigation training with the instructor in the forward cockpit. Particular attention has been given to providing all necessary functions, equipment and performance to allow USMC pilots efficient transition from basic V/STOL training to full operational AV-8B proficiency.

Excellent commonality with the AV-8B has been achieved. Improvement features designed into the AV-8B are retained. These include the supercritical

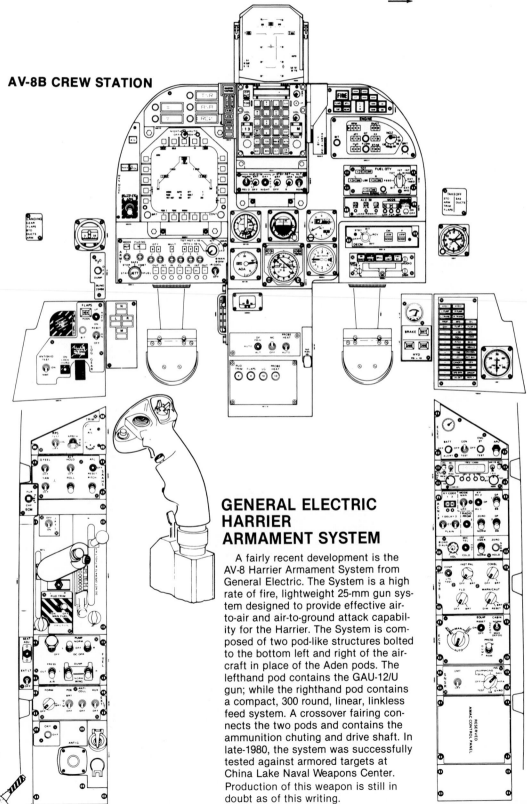

AV-8B CREW STATION

GENERAL ELECTRIC HARRIER ARMAMENT SYSTEM

A fairly recent development is the AV-8 Harrier Armament System from General Electric. The System is a high rate of fire, lightweight 25-mm gun system designed to provide effective air-to-air and air-to-ground attack capability for the Harrier. The System is composed of two pod-like structures bolted to the bottom left and right of the aircraft in place of the Aden pods. The lefthand pod contains the GAU-12/U gun; while the righthand pod contains a compact, 300 round, linear, linkless feed system. A crossover fairing connects the two pods and contains the ammunition chuting and drive shaft. In late-1980, the system was successfully tested against armored targets at China Lake Naval Weapons Center. Production of this weapon is still in doubt as of this writing.

wing, lift improvement devices, larger inlet, upgraded engine, composite structure, positive circulation flaps, and the Stabilization Augmentation and Attitude Hold System (SAAHS).

The principal areas of change are the forward fuselage and the raised vertical tail. Changes to the forward fuselage include moving the AV-8B cockpit forward 48.07 in. and down 6.61 in. to provide space to accommodate the second cockpit. The second cockpit is located such that its seat frame is 11.4 in. aft of the original AV-8B location. The aft cockpit provides the rear crew member with a forward view of 8.5° downwards on the centerline. This configuration results in the cockpits being in the same position relative to each other as on the TAV-8A. The forward and aft cockpits are the same size as the AV-8B cockpit except for a slight shortening of the aft cockpit to take advantage of the reduced rudder pedal forward adjustment. Contours are developed that retain the same windshield shape as the AV-8B, but with a different edge trim, and keep the AV-8B nose gear doors.

The other principal area of change, the vertical fin, has been enlarged to provide the necessary directional stability required due to the larger forward fuselage. Commonality in the design of the larger fin is provided by using the AV-8B fin and rudder mounted on a 17 in. extension attached to the aft fuselage. All other structure, including the wing, horizontal stabilator, and center and aft fuselage remain basically the same as the AV-8B, resulting in a configuration that provides maximum commonality and acceptable stability and control characteristics.

The TAV-8B like the AV-8B, has seven pylon stations for bombs, external fuel, or other stores, including air-to-air Sidewinder missiles. It can fly missions similar to the AV-8B and maintains the flexibility to operate from various types of air capable ships and land bases including austere forward sites. It carries one 25 mm gun. ARBS provides accurate day-night weapon delivery system.

THE AV-8C

The AV-8C is a logical and economical modification of the AV-8A. AV-8A operations have provided insight into aircraft improvements that the USMC feels would be worthwhile and cost effective. For example, the report of Marine AV-8A Operation Frosty Nozzle noted the lack of ECM equipment in the AV-8A. Marine operational exercise Palm Tree 2-77, in which the mission was to exercise fire support coordination in a

high threat surface-to-air and communications jammed environment, revealed the AV-8A to be particularly susceptible in this type of environment in that it possesses no RHAW indicators, no ECM equipment, and no secure voice communication.

THE AV-8C CILOP PROGRAM

In the AV-8C Conversion in Lieu of Procurement (CILOP) Program, AV-8As are converted to AV-8Cs by the incorporation of reliability, maintainability, and operational enhancement modifications that extend the aircraft's performance capability and improve survivability. The long range objective is to provide a total of 60 operational AV-8C aircraft by the end of 1984. The program will provide the U.S. Marine Corps with an aircraft that is capable of performing and surviving in the 1980s.

Several modifications in the last production buy of the AV-8A are to be incorporated during the program: improved hydraulic system, formation lights, and Continuously Computed Impact Point (CCIP) weapon delivery capability. Operational enhancement modifications include vertical takeoff Lift Improvement Devices (LIDS) and the ARC-159/KY-28 secure communciations, while survivability

The third of four full-scale developmental AV-8B's (161398) is shown during flight testing at Patuxent River in June, 1982. Scheme is green and grey, with black markings. *McDonnell Douglas photo C22-296-47*

Arriving just as we go to press, this beautiful photo shows AV-8B Number 2 (161397) in markings similar to those applied to the YAV-8B and AV-8C prototypes. This aircraft went to Edwards A.F.B. for engine and high angle-of-attack testing. Colors are red, black, gold, and white. *McDonnell Douglas photo C22-289-2*

70

modifications include an electronic countermeasures (ECM) suite.

The development portion of the CILOP Program is a three-phase effort aimed at defining the operational capability improvements (avionics and LIDS) scheduled for incorporation in AV-8C aircraft and verifying the operational capability improvements in AV-8A prototype aircraft. Each phase of the program is shown below:

PHASE	DURATION	TITLE
1	June 1978-Jan. 1980	Preproduction
2	June 1979-Feb. 1981	KIT VAL/VER
3	Aug.1981-	Production

Verification of the improvements will be accomplished by flight testing two AV-8As (158384, 158387) converted to the AV-8C configuration. Once verification and/or modification of the appropriate parts is accomplished, a kit to convert existing AV-8As to AV-8Cs will be designed and fitted to a third aircraft (158706) in order to validate specifications and conversion procedures. These procedures are then incorporated into the normal AV-8A refurbishment schedule.

AV-8C PROGRAM OBJECTIVES AND STATUS

AV-8C conversion efforts will be performed over a period of six years to ensure maintenance of an adequate light attack force level. Procurement of CILOP kits for incorporation by either MCAIR or NARF Cherry Point is programmed as follows:

Phase	Fiscal Year	Number of Kits	Installed by
Preproduction	1978/79	2 (Procured during VAL/VER)	MCAIR (1), NARF (1)
Production	1980	12	NARF
Production	1981	15	NARF
Production	1982	15	NARF
Production	1983	16	NARF
	Total	60	

The near-term AV-8C Program objective is for the Government to provide the required GFE and GSE to MCAIR and Naval Air Rework Facility (NARF), Cherry Point in the timely manner necessary to meet existing AV-8C development schedules. Where it is not possible to meet these schedules, work-around procedures or alternatives that minimize the impact on program schedule and cost must be developed.

Ultimately the AV-8C ECM suite will consist of an ALR-45F, APR-43, ALE-39, and ALQ-126. However, until sufficient ECM assets have been developed, approved, and produced, the AV-8C ECM suite will consist of an ALR-45, ALR-50, and ALE-39.

The T&E program for the AV-8C will be a two phased testing program to achieve increment levels of Approval for Service use (ASU) for the AV-8C. Phase I will address:
- LIDS
- Secure Communications (KY-28/ARC-159)
- Flare/Chaff (ALE-39)
- Antenna Patterns (ALR-45/45F)
Phase II will address:
- Radar Warning (ALR-45F/APR-43)
- DECM Pod (ALQ-126C)
- Weapons Delivery (CCIP/DIWAC)

AV-8C MODIFICATIONS

The AV-8C modifications are as follows:

1. AV-8A baseline plus SDLM modifications
- Aircraft 90 baseline

- FY 74 modifications

2. Reliability and maintainability modifications

3. Improved operational capability modifications

4. Performance capability modifications

RELIABILITY AND MAINTAINABILITY MODIFICATIONS: Reliability and maintainability predictions for the AV-8C are based on AV-8A service experience and the impact of changes incorporated in AV-8As to convert them to AV-8Cs. Data from the Navy 3M reporting system were used to establish AV-8A R&M values with 1974 chosen as a representative year. USMC AV-8As accumulated 10,900 flight hours during 1974. A detailed analysis of the experience has been conducted using a MCAIR computer program.

The baseline reliability and maintainability values for the AV-8A in 1974 are 1.5 Mean Flight Hours Between Failure (MFHBF) and 21.7 Direct Maintenance Man hours per Flight Hour (DMMH/FH). Thus, the AV-8C should have a 1.6 MFHBF (a net of 6.0% improvement) and 20.7 DMMH/FH (a net 4.8% improvement).

AV-8A TO AV-8C R&M CHANGE SUMMARY

MODIFICATIONS
Stencil Ejection Seat (MOD 613R8)
Outrigger Wheel Fork (MOD 955)
Yaw Autostab Actuator (MOD 758R2)
Water Contents Transmitter
12KVA,Electrical System (MOD 528R2)
Transformer-Rectifier Unit (MOD 751)
Hydraulic Filtration (ECP 0008R2)
Emergency Oxygen Cylinder (MOD 613R8)
ASN-116 AHRS (MOD 1009R1)
I/WAC (MOD 800R4)

TAV·8B

LEFT

AV·8C

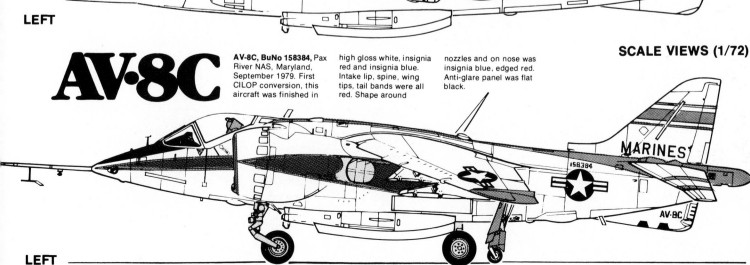

AV-8C, BuNo 158384, Pax River NAS, Maryland, September 1979. First CILOP conversion, this aircraft was finished in high gloss white, insignia red and insignia blue. Intake lip, spine, wing tips, tail bands were all red. Shape around nozzles and on nose was insignia blue, edged red. Anti-glare panel was flat black.

SCALE VIEWS (1/72)

MARINES
158384
AV·8C

LEFT

ADDED EQUIPMENT

Retractable Fence (LIDs)
Formation Lights (MOD 1011)
KY-28/TSEC Secure Voice
ARC-159 UHF Radio and Remote
  Indicator
Attitude Director Indictor
Horizontal Situation Indicator
Gun Pod Strakes
ALE-39 Flare/Chaff Dispenser
ALR-45F/APR-43 Radar Warning

DELETED EQUIPMENT

Ram Air Turbine Installation
Detachable Strakes
Ram Air Turbine
Fire Extinguisher System (MOD 889)
ARC-150 UHF Radio
Sound Recorder
ID-1329X Attitude Director Indicator
ID-1013A Horizontal Situation Indicator
Standby Sight
Nose Camera

AVIONICS MODIFICATIONS: Avionics improvements cover five basic areas. Some of the more important changes are discussed below.

KY-28 Secure Voice: Secure Voice capability will be provided by installing the KY-28 system. Aircraft provisions will be designed to allow operation with either the ARC-159 UHF or ARC-114 VHF radios. A cockpit switch will allow a selected radio to be encrypted. Control

The first of four full-scale developmental AV-8B's (BuNo 161396) is shown here on its maiden flight during checks of its roll, pitch, and yaw stability. *McDonnell Douglas photo C12-11328-68*

An interesting comparison shot of YAV-8B prototype number one (158394) and the first AV-8C CILOP aircraft (158384). Probably taken aboard the *U.S.S. Saipan* (LHA-2) during sea trials in late 1979. *McDonnell Douglas photo C12-8463-112*

logic will be designed to prevent simultaneous transmission of encrypted and plain language messages. Components are located in the nose and cockpit.

ARC-159 UHF radio: UHF Radio capability in the baseline AV-8A is provided by the 3500 channel ARC-150 (V)1. It is a panel mounted unit located in the right hand console behind the Communications Switch Unit. Pilots have reported the frequency/channel indicators to be difficult to read in flight. The ARC-150 (V)1 radio will be replaced by the 7000 channel ARC-159 UHF radio. The remote frequency/channel indicator will be mounted in a position to allow headup viewing by the pilot. System components are located in the cockpit.

Radar Warning (RWR): Radar warning capabilities will be provided by the ALR-45F and APR-43 warning receiver systems. The function of the RWR systems is to detect threat radars, identify them by comparing measured characteristics with known threat characteristics stored in the processor, determine the priority of each threat, and display the results of the pilot. These

Unusual view of AV-8C (BuNo. 158384) during hover/landing aboard carrier. In this photo, airplane is mounting two drop tanks and two LAU-61 2.75-inch rocket cannisters. Immense size of AV-8 intakes is readily apparent. *McDonnell Douglas photo C12-8463-224*

AV-8C EQUIPMENT INSTALLATION

RADAR WARNING BLANKING UNIT
APR-43 RADAR WARNING RECEIVER
ALR-45F RADAR WARNING PROCESSOR
UPPER C/D BAND OMNI ANTENNA
FRONT D.F. ANTENNA AND RECEIVER
AN/ARC-159 RADIO
REMOTE CHANNEL INDICATOR
ALE-39 CONTROL PANEL
KY-28 REMOTE UNIT
APR-43 ANTENNA ARRAY

REAR D.F. ANTENNAS AND RECEIVERS (2)
CHAFF DISPENSERS SEQUENCING SWITCHES
PROGRAMMER
ALQ-126C DECM POD
ANTENNA AND RECEIVER

CENTER CONSOLE:
• RADAR WARNING CONTROL
• RADAR WARNING CRT
• ALQ-126 DECM CONTROL

Prototype AV-8C (BuNo. 158384) approaches carrier deck for landing. Note extended airbrake, fully rotated engine exhaust nozzles, and hefty AV-8-type landing gear. Auxiliary intake doors are fully open. This aircraft was destroyed in a non-fatal accident in September, 1980. *McDonnell Douglas photo C12-8463-2*

systems use four quadrant antennas and four quadrant receiver units, and an APR-43 receiver, which uses a separate bottom mounted antenna array to perform various detection and direction finding functions. The ALR-45F cockpit control and CRT display will be installed in the cockpit. An interference blanker unit will be installed to provide blanking between all onboard systems. Changes to the wing tips and tail cone will be made to accommodate the antennas and receivers.

ALQ-126C Defensive Electronic Countermeasures (DECM) Pod: DECM threat emitter jamming capabilities will be provided by the ALQ-126D pod. The function of this missionized system is to receive threat emissions, electronically modify their characteristics, and to retransmit them in such a way that the enemy's probability of kill is degraded. This pod will be capable of operating in stand-alone or RWR assisted modes. The pod will be carried on the centerline station and operated by a control panel located on the center console in the cockpit.

Expendable Countermeasures: This capability will be provided by the ALE-39 system which dispenses chaff, flares or jammer expendable countermeasures upon command. Such commands are initiated either by the pilot or by the Radar Warning Receiver system depending on the mode selected. This system can carry 60 ECM canisters consisting of two groups of 20 and two groups of 10. The type of cannisters loaded into each group is selected prior to flight, based on the mission to be flown, and the group to be fired is selected by the pilot. The number of cannisters to be fired in a sequence and the interval between each is set up on the system programmer prior to flight. System components are located in the forward and aft fuselage. The lower moldline of the aft fuselage is modified to accept the dispenser installation.

PERFORMANCE MODIFICATIONS: Lift improvement devices, consisting of gun pod strakes and a retractable fence at the forward end of the gun pods, provide lift improvement in ground effect in the VTOL mode and reduce engine exhaust reingestion.

AV-8C CHARACTERISTICS

The major characteristics of the AV-8C are the same as those of the AV-8A. The power plant, store stations, guns, and external dimensions of the AV-8C are similar to the AV-8A. The only major physical changes in the AV-8C from the AV-8A are in the weight, electronics, and LIDs. The additional weight essentially consists of the LIDs. Each AV-8C aircraft when modified, will have a weight empty which is greater than the original weight empty of the AV-8A from which it was transformed. The weight difference will cause minimal differences between the performance of the AV-8C and the performance of the AV-8A aircraft.

Weapon loading capabilities are effectively the same as on the AV-8A except for the increased V/STOL lift capability resulting from the LID.

AV-8A — AV-8C WEIGHTS *(LB)*	AV-8A	WEIGHT CHANGE	AV-8C
Weight Empty	11,890	+197	12,087
Operating Weight Empty	12,131	+145	12,336
Basic Flight Design Gross Weight	20,600	0	20,600
Maximum Takeoff Gross Weight			
STO	24,600	0	24,600
VTO	17,050	+1,100	18,150

Prototype AV-8C, BuNo. 158384, one of two CILOP revamped AV-8As, lifts from the deck of *U.S.S. Saipan* (LHA-2) during sea trials. *McDonnell Douglas photo C12-8463-319*

Prototype AV-8C (BuNo. 158384) is shown immediately prior to takeoff from carrier deck. Note this airplane's unique color scheme which superficially resembles that of the AV-8B prototypes. Note also the gun canoe mounted ventral fin-like devices unique to this AV-8 model. *McDonnell Douglas photo C12-8463-70*

Future DEVELOPMENT

A decade of operational service accumulated with the Royal Air Force, the United States Marine Corps and the Spanish Navy has demonstrated beyond doubt the tactical and strategic importance of the vectored-thrust V/STOL light attack weapons system. That the AV-8A Harrier is not a supersonic aircraft makes that achievement even more significant. However, it is a record which does not make supersonic vectored-thrust V/STOL any less desirable.

Fully supersonic applications present different problems and the higher thrust requirements are normally achieved by afterburning in conventional military turbofans. This was anticipated as early as 1961 by Rolls Royce, when it tested and proved plenum chamber burning (PCB) in the BS100 engine. The Pegasus, because of its unique feature of exhausting the bypass flow and the hot flow separately through pairs of rotating nozzles, enables thrust boosting to be obtained by burning fuel in the plenum chamber which supplies the cold nozzles. This is the PCB system. The BS100 engine was conceived and built for the ill-fated Hawker P.1154 aircraft, which was to be a supersonic attack fighter with a Mach 2 capability. The P.1154 was cancelled in 1965, but not before the BS100 had run at its rated thrust of over 30,000 lbs. In 1964 and 1965 the BS100 ran successfully with the incorporation of the low-loss drooped and trailed nozzle layout.

In 1974 considerable design work was done both in the U.S. and U.K. on more advanced versions of the Harrier using a derivative of the Pegasus 11 known as the Pegasus 15. The designation of these aircraft, which were studied in both subsonic and supersonic form was AV-16 and AV-16 S-6 respectively. Also known as the AV-8X, this was to be the "advanced" Harrier. The AV-16 series was finally abandoned in 1976 in favor of a more limited objective — the AV-8B.

The most recent advances, as of early 1981, include the proposed joint development of a supersonic V/STOL fighter with a related flight demonstration program. This is being promoted by McDonnell Douglas and Rolls-Royce. The U.S. Navy, the U.S. Air Force, the Royal Air Force, the Royal Navy, and the National Aeronautics and Space Administration are all suggested participants.

This proposed supersonic V/STOL program is considered by many industry and DoD officials to be the next logical step in the AV-8 story. The proposed flight demonstration airplane, in fact, is known as the AV-8SX (Supersonic EXperimental). It is proposed that it be based on a modified AV-8A airframe that incorporates the aforementioned PCB version of the Pegasus. This engine, known as the Pegasus II, would offer a thrust increase of over 50%.

The AV-8SX is expected to be a four to five year program costing between $300 and $500-million. Performance increases resulting from the program would include a maximum Mach number of 1.6. Over-all performance improvements would provide the AV-8SX

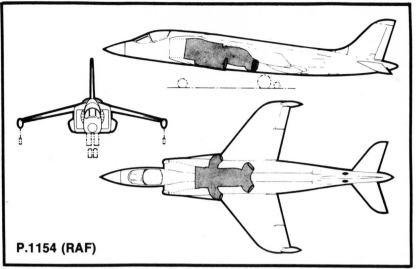

P.1154 (RAF)

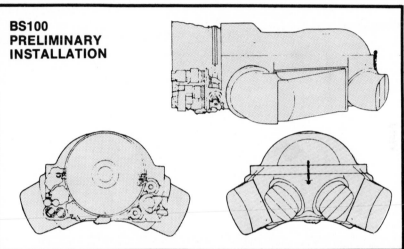

BS100 PRELIMINARY INSTALLATION

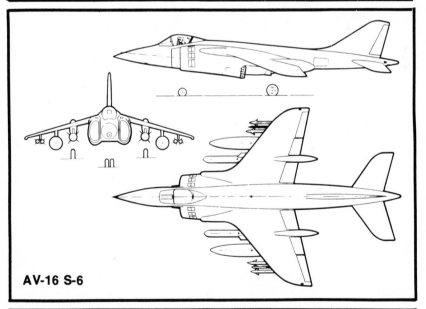

AV-16 S-6

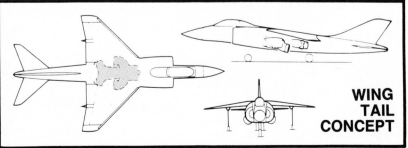

WING TAIL CONCEPT

with capabilities similar, in most respects, to that of the General Dynamics F-16. In many areas the airplane would actually be capable of outperforming the F-16. Among these would be short field capability, inflight maneuverability, and weapons related avionics.

The AV-8SX potential also implies significant improvements in close air support, interdiction, and other related roles. These would be possible through the additional 4,000 pounds thrust that would be provided by the AV-8SX's improved Pegasus engine.

Many of the proposed AV-8SX improvements are currently being funded by the U.S. Marine Corps and McDonnell Douglas under programs related to the upcoming AV-8B Plus. The latter is a significantly improved AV-8B that offers all-weather weapons delivery (via the inclusion of the Hughes APG-65 radar now used in the McDonnell Douglas F-18) and the higher thrust Pegasus 11F-35 engine. It has been proposed that both the U.S. Navy and the U.S. Marine Corps acquire the airplane.

The Pegasus 11F-35 is derived from the Pegasus 11-21 (F402-RR-402) engine used in the AV-8B. Modifications include a new fan, zero scarf front nozzles, turbine exhaust diffuser, and a modified accessory gearbox. Maximum thrust is over 25,000 pounds.

It has also been proposed by Rolls Royce that the standard Pegasus 11-21, currently rated at 21,500 pounds thrust, be uprated to 30,000 pounds. This would be accomplished through PCB. It is also being proposed that the new Pegasus 11-35 also be equipped with PCB, this increasing thrust from 25,000 pounds to over 35,000 pounds.

Research continues in the areas of more powerful engines and more sophisticated airframe designs. High-performance V/STOL combat capability is considered by many modern military strategists as an essential tool. Creating supersonic V/STOL is not a question of technology — it's more a question of time and money. ∎

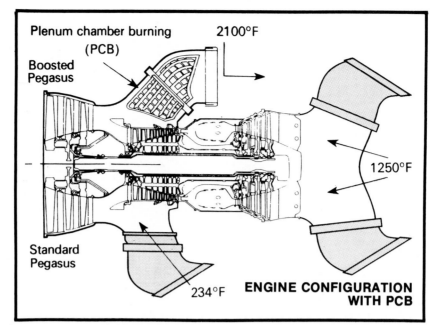

ENGINE CONFIGURATION WITH PCB

Plenum chamber burning (PCB)
Boosted Pegasus
2100°F
1250°F
Standard Pegasus
234°F

FUTURE PEGASUS PCB CONFIGURATION

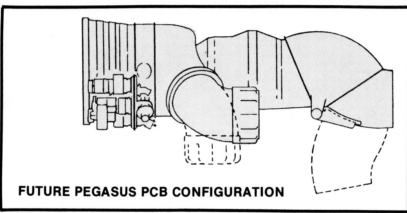

3-NOZZLE AUGMENTED VECTORED-THRUST SUPERSONIC V/STOL DESIGN PROPOSAL

Low altitude hover capability is demonstrated by this VMA-231 AV-8A (BuNo. 158393). Note extension of main and nose landing gear in "unloaded" state. *British Aerospace photo 733981*

Modeling

THE KESTREL AND HARRIER: AN OVERVIEW OF AVAILABLE KITS

The AV-8/Harrier is a unique aircraft, one fortunately recognized by the world's kit manufacturers as having considerable sales potential. Kits of the Harrier have been issued in every accepted aircraft scale except 1/100th, and there are at least two conversion kits and several custom decal sheets available to the serious modeler. What we would like to do here is give those of you interested in building a replica of the AV-8 an idea of the materials available to you. A truly detailed study of each kit would take more space than we have available in this publication, but you should at least be able to choose a kit to work with from the information provided here. Please remember that your best guide to building a good model is one based on primary sources, particularly photographs. Choose the aircraft that you wish to model, acquire the references to enable you to do the job correctly, and enjoy yourself.

P.1127/Kestrel

To date there is only one kit of the Harrier prototype, an ancient offering by Airfix. As far as we know it is no longer available, which is probably just as well since it's a prime example of Airfix's practice of issuing kits of prototype aircraft based on press releases and speculation rather than fact. The kit is more or less an early P.1127, complete with the small, neutral-position horizontal tailplane. It features poor detailing, lots of rivets, and is unfortunately the only game in town if you want to build a prototype. On the bright side, the P.1127 and the Kestrel were two quite different aircraft, and you could convert an AV-8 to Kestrel/XV-6A standards fairly easily. Building this kit as what it's supposed to be, a P.1127 (early variant) is feasible if you want a representative type rather than a 100% accurate scale model. As a final note, the kit's decals are for XP972, while the artwork on the packaging is for XP831, which sums up Airfix's approach to this kit rather nicely, we think.

AV-8A

To date every kit of the AV-8/Harrier released by anybody has been of this variant, which is logical considering the age of most of them. Some of these kits are really good, and some are really poor, but each of the commonly-built scales has at least one de-

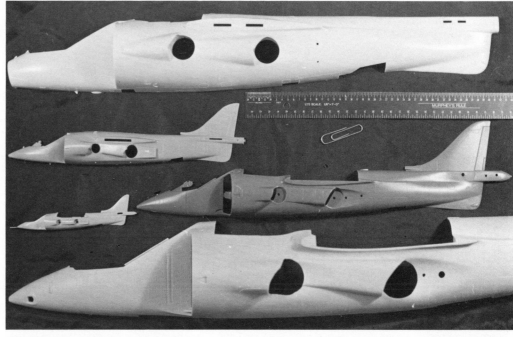

cent Harrier available to it. Here is a look at what's currently available (September 1982) from the smallest to the largest. Remember, these kits are all of the "A" model, although an AV-8C should be a pretty simple proposition since it's essentially an uprated AV-8A. If you want an AV-8B we strongly suggest that you wait for someone to release a kit of it because the conversion would most emphatically *not* be a simple one.

1/144th Scale

There are two kits available in this scale, Crown's No. P803 and Revell's No. 1045. There isn't much point in choosing one over the other because they're both the same kit, the only real difference being the decals, which are offered with both RAF and USMC markings in the Revell kit and RAF only in the Crown model. They are equally poor decals and need to be replaced no matter who's name is on the box. The kit(s) themselves aren't bad, and build up into effective AV-8 models if you're ready to accept the detailing problems caused by their size (or lack of it). Ordnance is strictly English and should be replaced by something a bit more in keeping with

American usage. As a passing note, the Crown kit is marketed as a GR.*3*, which it definitely is not.

1/72 Scale

Airfix "Harrier", No. 266.

This kit is the oldest of the Harriers, being a direct descendent of the Airfix P.1127. It isn't too bad if you don't have anything else available, but shows its age in a number of ways including poor detailing, raised control surfaces, a nose that's a bit undersized, poor decals, a poor canopy, and on, and on, and . . . On the plus side, the underwing stores are probably the best available in this scale although they're really only applicable to aircraft in RAF service. You can work with this kit if the situation demands it, but there are better available.

Hasegawa "Hawker Siddeley Harrier", No. JS-028.

Hasegawa hasn't always turned out kits as good as its F-14, but they have usually managed to give us a product that is at least usable. Their Harrier is quite a few cuts above that, and is easily the best in 1/72nd scale. It does feature a number of detail omissions and gives the exhaust nozzles as two-piece assemblies, which will cause you untold grief during assembly. Fuselage construction is another joy, offering seams in some really hard-to-get-at places, but the model is essentially accurate and is very nicely mold-

With Murphy's Rule to guide you...here are specimens of the various scales: at top - 1/32 scale Revell's kit; at bottom is Airfix's 1/24 scale offering; at left is Airfix's 1/72 version and Crown's 1/144 kit; and in the center, Monogram's quarter-scale gem.

ed. The horizontal stabs are a bit small but can be replaced, and you'll have to add a camera port in the nose (none of the other kits in this scale have it either, except for the Airfix model which gives you a port on *both* sides of the nose when it should only be in the left). Underwing stores are well done but again are only useful for a British aircraft. Drops are provided and, at least in the older kits, decals are just about worthless. Bad points notwithstanding, this is the kit to work with if you build to 1/72nd. Your Hasegawa F-4 didn't need all that ordnance anyway!

Frog/Rovex, kit No. not known.

At one point in the early seventies Hasegawa and Frog had an arrangement by which each imported and, in some cases, produced each other's models. Frog's Harrier is an example of this, being a reboxed Hasegawa kit with improved decals. We wouldn't even advise looking for the Frog issue unless you happen to be a kit collector because there is absolutely no difference between the two kits except for decals and packaging. Build it if you've got it and forget it if you don't.

Matchbox "HS Mk-1 Harrier", No. PK-16.
AMT "Hawker Siddeley AV-8A Harrier", No. 7112.

These are, as you would guess, the same kit. Matchbox (Lesney) has a well deserved reputation for doing the best Between-The-Wars biplanes in the world. They deserve that reputation. They also, somewhat unfortunately, have another reputation, equally deserved, for doing some of the worst jets in the entire world of scale modeling. Lesney's mold makers *did* have an understanding of the way a Harrier's undercarriage landing gear functions, but that's about all they did well. We wouldn't hesitate to build this kit if it were the only one available, but it isn't and we'd really have to relegate this particular offering (in either of its guises) to a second or possibly third choice behind the Hasegawa model. It's poorly detailed, has a poor canopy, and features surface detailing ("scribing" is a term that almost comes to mind) that resembles the latticework of canals once so prominent in America's northeastern regions. We hate to be so negative, but this is (these are?) a really poor kit when compared to most of the others. We would suggest leaving it alone unless you just don't have any other choice.

Lindberg "Harrier British Jet Airplane", No. 980, No. 948

Yes, Lindberg has a kit of the AV-8A — sort of. It's a snap-tight kit, it isn't to 1/72nd, it's a terrible scale model, and is probably one of the most de-

tailed (albeit incorrectly) toys your kids will ever have to play with. It's true that the Lindberg of our youth (for those of us who were kids in the 1950s) made some excellent models from time to time, but this isn't the fifties and this kit is far from excellent. Still, it has a place in the modeling world, and we rather suspect that Lindberg never meant to compete with Hasegawa anyway. Give this one to your kids and let them enjoy themselves with it — it's a lot better than most of the models we cut *our* teeth on. (You might want prefer to buy Kit No. 948 if you have the chance — its decals are just as poor as those in No. 980 but they're of the dry transfer sort; it's a really nice innovation in a somewhat questionable kit.)

1/48th Scale

Tamiya "Hawker Siddeley Harrier GR. Mk. 1", No. MA112.

Tamiya has a well-deserved reputation for doing things right and this is one of the kits they made that reputation on. It builds up very easily and produces an accurate AV-8 that requires additional detailing on the part of its builder. This model was *the* Harrier kit of its day and close examination reveals the reasons why — fine detailing, generally accurate components, a good representation of the AV-8's landing gear, good ordnance (albeit British), and a complete set of decals for three different aircraft. Problem areas include a huge hole in the top of the fuselage so that you can display a minimally-detailed engine, no interior detail to speak of, and intakes/ducts not nearly up to the standard of the rest of the kit. They also did the landing gear doors incorrectly and left off a number of small vents and ducts. Still, there's nothing so wrong with this kit that it can't be made into a beautiful model with a negligible amount of work.

Monogram "Hawker Harrier", No. 5420.

It really isn't fair to compare this kit against its only quarter-scale competition, the Tamiya GR.1, but that's the way things shape up and, on the whole, the Monogram kit is far the superior of the two. (But then they had several years worth of advantage over Tamiya, whose kit dates back to the early seventies.) Detailing is better and generally more accurate, *American* stores are provided, although you should possibly be aware of the fact that the real AV-8 can carry more than two bombs and two AIM-9Ls at one time. The best Aden gun pods in the business are provided, and the kit is generally beyond reproach if you disregard the fact that somebody forget to provide for the camera port on the left side of the nose. Some of the pieces don't fit very well (an unfortunate Monogram trademark of sorts) and the kit decals will literally curl up and fall off the model if you attempt to use Solveset on them. They also happen to be much too thick, but most of the AV-8's markings can be pieced together from odds and ends in your

spares box anyway. As a final unkind note, the kit's box art shows an AV-8A from VMAT-203 in the process of launching, You will note that the little vent doors on the sides of the intakes are in their "parade rest" location — those at the top hanging open and those at the sides and on the bottom partially or completely closed. This is a normal condition for these doors when the engine isn't running, but you won't see it this way when everything is working. This won't really affect your model one way or another, but we thought you might want to know about it. Other than these one or two minor problems we would suggest that you build the Monogram kit if your tastes run to 1/48th scale. There are a couple of minor things wrong with it but it's essentially the best of the two kits in its scale and is probably the best of all the Harrier kits.

1/32nd Scale

Revell "Hawker Siddeley Harrier "Jump Jet", No. H-248.

This is the kit of choice if you happen to model in 1/32nd scale, mainly because it's the *only* kit in 1/32nd scale. It's fairly old (mid-seventies) and a bit hard to find these days although the Falklands business may well change that, but it's essentially a good kit and is worth the effort you'll need to put into it in order to get an acceptable model. It's biggest failing is Revell's typical "unfinished" molding. All of the shapes are there, as is most of the detailing you'll want, but a lot of things are oversimplified and will need some help if you want them to look right. The interior, gear doors, pylons, weapons (British again), landing gear, all will need work. There's an engine included, which isn't really very good and should probably be removed and introduced to your trash can, and the fuselage accordingly features a large hole in its upper decking which you'll probably want to delete. Kit decals are usable and nicely printed though a little thick, and you're pretty much limited to what the kit gives you unless you can make your own (fortunately not that big a deal on the AV-8 since most of the markings are fairly simple). If you can find this kit at a reasonable (non-scalpers) price we'd definitely recommend it to you — it's a potentially excellent model just waiting for a home.

1/24th Scale

Airfix "Hawker Harrier", No. 18001-4.

This is probably THE Harrier kit if you've got the room to display it. Until the advent of the Monogram model this one was the best-detailed of all of the AV-8s on the market; it's still far and away the most impressive. It has an engine, and it's a good one, very much a model in itself without much detailing left for you to add. External detailing is generally excellent, although not as good as Monogram's, and you won't have to do much to the kit except carefully build it. It even includes the extended wingtips sometimes used by the RAF for ferry purposes, if your tastes run to that sort of thing. Our major complaint concerning this model is the surface finish of most of the exterior components — for some reason Airfix put a slight texture on just about every large external surface and the fine-grained paints currently available to the American modeler will not hide it. That means that you'll probably want to sand *all* of the exterior smooth, and it'll take quite a bit of time (and more than a little care) to do that. We also don't much like the All-Pictures instruction sheet; we don't think it gives the inexperienced modeler much of a chance. (But then, how many neophytes start off building $30.00 models?) The decals are also on the poor side — typically Airfix which means virtually unusable, but the model is large

enough for you to be able to cut stencils and paint on most of the markings if you've got the ambition to do that. These problems are minor, however, and the Airfix Harrier could easily be the Best of all the Harriers — it's certainly the most impressive. Just take your time with it and give it the extra attention that it deserves.

Conversion Kits

There are two conversion kits to alter the 1/72nd scale GR. 1 kits to T.2 standards that are worth having (there may well be others lurking out there someplace but these two are *usable,* which is more than we can say about a lot of the vacuum-formed "conversions" currently offered by scale modeling's garage industry). Both of these kits are injection-molded and both are going to be a bit difficult to obtain, although one or the other is the only way to go if you want a TAV-8A.

AIR Conversions No. 2, "Hawker Siddeley Harrier T2."

This is the first of the injection-molded trainer conversions, having originally been issued in the mid-1970s. It will be pretty hard to find but is worth the effort since it's the better of the two. A new nose and tail are given, along with a good canopy and an excellent instruction sheet by Richard Ward of ModelDecal fame. All of the pieces more-or-less fit together and the completed conversion looks extremely convincing once some detail has been added. No interior is provided and cockpit sill/coaming detail is nonexistent, but this is the kit we'd choose if we were building a TAV-8A.

Pegasus No. 001 "Hawker Siddeley Harrier T.2"

This is the most recent of the AV-8 conversion kits and is perfectly usable if you cant find the AIR kit. The principal drawbacks are poor instructions and a thick, hazy canopy. An attempt has been made to provide some of the instrument shrouding for each cockpit, and all of the parts are of a consistently high quality except for the canopy and vertical tail. We've done a fair amount of work with the AIR kit and haven't been able to work with this one at all, since we borrowed it and have to give it back to its rightful owner. Still, we think it would be a simple matter to get a good model from it, although the kit's instructions advise using the Airfix Harrier and we tend to disagree with that, much preferring the Hasegawa offering.

General Modeling Notes

Most of the kits we've discussed here will produce an adequate model of the AV-8A or C if properly built. All of them have at least one or two minor problems, but things that bother us (such as removable panels) may not concern you at all. There are, however, a couple of things you need to watch out for on nearly all of the kits if you want your model to be completely accurate (within reason, of course — we don't personally belong to the "it's ½mm too long" school; if you do you're certainly welcome to cut and chop to your heart's content).

Exhausts: Most of the kits currently available fall down badly in this area. We suggest either rebuilding or replacing as required, because you'll never get the seams out of the two-piece ducts that many of these kits feature.

Intake Vents: You have a major problem here — all of the kits indicate these vents, but none of them really do it right. Essentially, these vents are little doors, and they work off of intake pressure. If the aircraft is parked, with the engine not running, the doors that can hang down into the fuselage will be doing just that, with the doors just below them partially open and those on the undersides of the aircraft completely closed. With the engine running, all of the vents can be open or closed, but they will all be doing the same thing, whatever that may be. (As a rule they're open when the aircraft is hovering or taxiing and closed in conventional forward flight.) We would suggest that you choose a situation for your model to portray and approach the intakes from that point of view.

Canopy: Most of the kits have a reasonably accurate canopy, but the framing takes a bite out of the sides of the rear fuselage and most of the available models don't portray this. It's really only noticeable when the canopy is open, but it will still be a problem and should be corrected.

Landing Gear: Watch out for the doors on the main gear. They are generally closed, not open, and your model should be portrayed that way unless it is either a) in the process of retracting its gear, or b) being serviced.

Camera Port: The camera in the left side of the nose may or may not be installed, but the port will be there no matter what. It has to be added to those kits that don't have it, and is, again, ONLY found on the port side. If you happen to be building a kit that has a camera port on the starboard side (*a la* Airfix) it must be deleted.

Radio Mast: Most of these kits don't have one and the real AV-8 generally does. You'll need to add it if your kit doesn't furnish it.

Gun Pods: These pods are a feature of most USMC Harriers. If a particular aircraft doesn't use them it will have ventral strakes fitted in their place, and it's entirely possible to find an aircraft asymetrically fitted, with one pod and one strake. If your model has the pods they will probably require extensive modification, since only the Monogram and 1/24th scale Airfix kits give decent representations of them.

Ordnance: This particular comment may almost seem unnecessary but you should remember that the AV-8A/C is an American service aircraft and as such generally operates with American bombs and rockets, although it can use NATO ordnance if required (the Air Force used some of it in Viet Nam if you'll recall). A lot of the kits provide RAF/NATO weapons and you should be careful of what ends up hanging from your model.

Detailing: Most of the kits available to us will require at least some degree of detailing; a few of them will require quite a bit of it. Rather than impose a lengthy "every-nut-and-bolt" article on you we'll suggest that you study the photographs in this work and detail accordingly. There have been few changes to the basic AV-8A/C airframe since its service introduction and most of the omissions suffered by the various kits are easily correctable and can be made from careful research of available photos. In the case of the Monogram and large Airfix kits there really isn't much to add anyway, but any of the 1/72nd scale kits can stand a little detail. It's your choice.

A LOOK AT DECALS

1/144th Scale

Kit:	US Markings	RAF Markings	Comment
Crown	None	233 Sqdn (OCU)	Very poor
Revell	VMA-513	233 Sqdn (OCU)	Very Poor

Custom Decals: No custom decals are available in this scale.

1/72nd Scale

Kit:	US Markings	RAF Markings	Comment
P.1127	None	General	Marked for XP972
Airfix	None	General	Marked for XV738, no squadron.
Hasegawa	None (early release)	General	Marked for XV738 or XV739, no Sqdn allocation
AMT/ Lesney	VMA-513	No. 3 Sqdn.	
Lindberg	None	General	"027" (*Kit Release #948 has dry transfer decals)

1/48th Scale:

Kit:	US Markings	RAF Markings	Comment
Tamiya	VMA-513	No. 1, No. 4, and No. 20 Sqdn.	Glossy and should be replaced but can be used if you have no other choice.
Monogram	VMAT-203	No. 1 Sqdn.	Difficult to work with and much too thick, but a nice effort on the VMAT-203 machine.

Custom Decals: There are no custom decals in this scale.

1/32nd Scale:

Kit:	US Markings	RAF Markings	Comment
Revell	VMA-513	No. 1 Sqdn	Not bad for kit decals, usable.

Custom Decals: There aren't any available in 1/32nd scale.

1/24th Scale:

Kit:	US Markings	RAF Markings	Comment
Airfix	VMA-513,	No. 1 Sqdn.	Very accurate but glossy and of very poor quality.

Custom Decals: Today, all of the custom Harrier decals have been done to 1/72nd scale, primarily from Modeldecal of England but more recently by MicroScale as well. The ModelDecal sheets are generally of excellent quality but are almost entirely limited to RAF subjects, while the MicroScale offering include both the AV-8A and, on a separate sheet, the Sea Harrier. These sheets cover the following subjects:

Model Decals:
No. 7:   Covers No. 1 Sqdn, RAF, ca.

1969. Includes markings for the GR.1 that participated in the TransAtlantic Race.
No. 11:   This sheet features two Harriers from RAF Germany, from No. 20 and No. 45 Sqdn., both ca. 1971.
No. 15:   This is the only AV-8 offered by ModelDecal, from VMA-513, ca. 1971/72.
No. 23:   An aircraft from No. 3 Sqdn. RAF Germany, is featured here, from mid-1973.

Modeldecal produce one of the most accurate products available to the serious scale modeler, although they are sometimes difficult to obtain and are thicker than those of Microscale. It should also be noted that they are a often keyed to the use of kit national insignia and stenciling although this is much more prevalent on the earlier releases than on their later efforts. You should also note that these decal sheets are not entirely devoted to the Harrier or AV-8A; each sheet contains several subjects of which the Harrier is just one.

MicroScale:

No. 72-355:   "U.S. Marine Hawker Siddeley AV-8A Harriers VMA-531 (sic), VMA-513, VMA-231, and VMA-542."

The AV-8A filled an important slot in Marine Corps aviation for the past several years, and the early total lack of markings for them has always puzzled us. MicroScale has finally done something about that with this decal sheet and it's now possible to model all of the AV-8A squadrons except for VMAT-203 from off-the-shelf accessory decals.

As is usual with Krasel's products, the quality on this sheet is excellent, at least in regard to the various squadron markings and stencilling. Complete schemes are provided for four different aircraft; two from VMA-513 (mis-identified on the instruction sheet as -531, although the decals are correct) and one each from -231 and -542. All of the schemes provided are

colorful and accurate, and are complimented by some excellent stencilling. Unfortunately, the national insignia aren't nearly so good and should be replaced — we also wonder why no low-vis schemes were provided, although we admit that most Harriers don't have much color on them and these *are* extremely colorful. This sheet is highly recommended to the serious modeler. Its instruction sheet, unfortunately, is not.

MicroScale's reputation for printing the best decals in the business is well deserved; so is their reputation for doing the worst instruction sheets in the business. This one features a drawing of a Sea Harrier for stencil placement and muddy, poorly-defined AV-8 drawings for the squadron markings. It's a shame that such good decals are marred by an instruction sheet of this sort, because anyone without references is going to have problems. We know the markings are correct, but it's easy to see a credibility problem in the making — if the instructions are this poor, can you really trust the decals? We do, but then we weren't limited to just refering to the instruction sheet either.

Modeling the AV-8B

The AV-8B is a totally different aircraft from either the AV-8A or AV-8C and, quite honestly, you can't get there from here. Working up a B model would entail a *lot* more work than meets the eye, and we would prefer to wait for someone to produce a kit of it once it's entered squadron service.

Modeling the AV-8C

If you're interested in doing an AV-8C you're in for the treat of your modeling career, because there are no exterior differences between the A and C models except for the Lift Improvement Devices (known as LID) on the undersurface of the aircraft. These essentially consist of fixed strakes on the gun packs and a deployable transverse fence just aft of the nose gear. Add these, mark accordingly, and you've got an AV-8C.

Unusual markings adorn this AV-8A (BuNo. 159961) of VMA-513. Of particular note are the medium blue rudder with white stars, and the tail code and nose number in the same medium blue. All other lettering in black. Dated 27 May 1976 this photo was shot at Quantico, Virginia. *U.S. Marine Corps photo A569050 by R.L. Elmore*

Production

MODEL	SERIAL NO.	QUANTITY	FIRST FLIGHT	NOTES
AV-8A	158384/395	12	Sept. 1970	Handed over 11/20/70; Block 1
AV-8A	158694/711	18	?	Block 1
AV-8A	158948/977	30	?	Block 2
AV-8A	159230/¼459	30	?	Block 3
AV-8A	159366/377	12	?	Block 4
TAV-8A	159378/385	8	?	Block 4
AV-8A (SP)*	159557/562	6	Feb. 1976	
AV-8A (SP)*	161174/178	5	?	
TAV-8A (SP)*	159563/564	2	1976	
YAV-8B	158394, 158395	(2)***	Nov. 9, 1980	Ordered July 28, 1976
AV-8C	158384, 158387, 158706	(3)***	May 5, 1979	
AV-8B**	161396/399	4	Nov. 5, 1981	FSD Prototypes

*Bought via U.S. Marine Corps and delivered to Spanish *Arma Aerea de la Armada* (Spanish Navy).
**FSD procurement to serve as pre-production prototypes for production AV-8B.   ***Converted AV-8A airframes.

Specification Tables

(data in italics is estimated)

	XV-6A	AV-8A	TAV-8A	AV-8B	TAV-8B	AV-8C
Wing span (combat)	22'11''	25'3''	25'3''	30'4''	30'4''	25'3''
Wing span (ferry)	na	29'8''	29'8''	na	na	29'8''
Wing sweepback	*40 deg.*	35.17 deg.	35.17 deg.	*37 deg.*	*37 deg.*	35.17 deg.
Wing chord (root)	*10'*	11'8''	11'8''	11'6''	11'6''	11'8''
Wing chord (tip)	*4'6''*	4'2''	4'2''	3'7''	3'7''	4'2''
Wing anhedral	*12 deg.*	12 deg.	12 deg.	12 deg.	12 deg.	12 deg.
Wing aspect ratio (combat)	?	3.175	3.175			3.175
Wing aspect ratio (ferry)	na	4.08	4.08	na	na	4.08
Wing incidence		1.75 deg.	1.75 deg.	3 deg.	3 deg.	1.75 deg.
Length (overall)	42'6''	45'6''	55'11''	46'4''	50'4''	45'6''
Height (overall)	10'9''	11'4''	13'8''	12'	13'7''	11'4''
Tailplane span	13'10''	13'11''	13'11''	*13'11''*	*13'11''*	13'11''
Outrigger Wheel Track	*22'2''*	22'2''	22'2''	16'7''	16'7''	22'22''
Wheelbase (nose to main)	*12'*	11'4''	11'4''	*11'5''*	*11'5''*	11'4''
Gross Wing Area (combat) sq. ft.	*186*	201.1	201.1	230	230	201.1
Gross Wing Area (ferry) sq. ft.	na	216	216	na	na	216
Aileron Area (side) sq. ft.	*5.1*	5.25	5.25	6.19	6.19	5.25
Flap Area, sq. ft.	*14*	13.9	13.9	15.49	15.49	13.9
Fin Area (except ventral) sq. ft.	23.5	25.8	38.4	*26.5*	*39.44*	25.8
Rudder Area, sq. ft.	5.3	5.3	5.3	5.23	5.23	5.3
Tailplane Area, sq. ft.	47.6	47.5	47.5	48.5	?	47.5
Tailplane Anhedral	*16 deg.*	15.8 deg.	15.8 deg.	*15.8 deg.*	*15.8 deg.*	15.8 deg.
Empty Weight, pounds	*10,000*	11,890	13,000	12,473	?	12,087
Operating Empty Weight, pounds	*10,400*	12,191	13,750	12,750	?	12,336
Basic Flight Design Gross Weight	*15,000*	20,600		22,950	?	20,600
Maximum Takeoff Gross Weight, pounds: STOL	15,500	24,600		29,750	?	24,600
VTOL	12,400	17,050		19,185	?	12,400
Maximum speed (low altitude)	660 mph	737 mph	700 mph	750 mph	700 mph	730 mph
Maximum Mach Number (dive)	1.02	1.27	1.1	1.25	1.2	1.25
Service Ceiling, ft.	50,000	52,000	50,000	55,000	53,000	52,000
Max. Ferry Range	na	1,750 mi.	1,750 mi.	2,460 mi.	2,460 mi.	1,750 mi.
Powerplant	Pegasus 5	402-RR-402 Pegasus II	402-RR-402 Pegasus II	402-RR-405 Pegasus II	402-RR-405 Pegasus II	402-RR-402 Pegasus II
Static Thrust	15,200	19,000	19,000	21,800	21,800	19,000
Internal Fuel (U.S. gallons)	759	759	759	1,103	1,103	759
External Fuel (U.S. gallons)	2 x 100 (approx.)	2x111.5 or 2x280	2x111.5 or 2x280	2x111.5 or 2x280	2x111.5 or 2x280	2x111.5 or 2x280

BIBLIOGRAPHY:

AV-8A — A New Dimension in Readiness. USMC document, June, 1974.

AV-8B — Executive Summary. McDonnell Douglas, June, 1978.

AV-8B/The Marine Machine. McDonnell Douglas

AV-8B — The Next Step. McDonnell Douglas

AV-8B — Performance Plus. McDonnell Douglas, August, 1978.

Berliner, Don. "Marines' New VTOL Harrier", *Air Trails Military Aircraft,* 1971, p. 66.

Blot, Harry W. "Fly, Hover and Fight", *British Aerospace Quarterly,* April, 1980. pp. 2-8. Originally appeared in *Air Force* Magazine.

Blot, Harry W. "A New Dimension in Air Combat", *The Rolls-Royce Magazine,* Number Six, pp. 3-8.

Brown, Kevin. "The Plane That Makes Airfields Obsolete",*Popular Mechanics,* June 1, 1970, pp. 80-83 + .

Coles, Bob. "Sea Harrier", *Air Combat,* Vol. 5/No. 4, July, 1977, pp. 20-35 + .

Cooper, Bert. *The British Harrier V/STOL Aircraft,* Congressional Research Service, Report No. 81-18OF, The Library of Congress, 15 August, 1981.

Cooper, Bert. *V/STOL Aircraft Development,* Issue Brief Number IB78020, Congressional Research Service, Library of Congress, September, 1978.

Cooper, Bert. *V/STOL Developments: Background and Status,* Report No. 78-51F, Congressional Research Service, Library of Congress, June 1, 1979.

"Designing The Pegasus", *Fight International,* 19 October, 1972.

Development of the Pegasus — 1957-1978, Rolls-Royce Ltd. TS 3059, December, 1978.

Elliott, John M. *An Interview with Tom Miller* (LT GEN, USMC, Ret).

Farley, John. "Sea Harrier", *Navy International,* February, 1976, pp. 10-25.

Final Report of the Defense Science Board Task Force on V/STOL Aircraft, Department of Defense, November, 1979.

Fozard, J.W. "Sea Harrier", *The Aeronautical Journal,* January, 1977, pp. 14-40.

Fozard, J.W. "Ski-Jump — A Great Leap for Tactical Airpower", *British Aerospace Paper 79-0696,* April, 1980, pp. 2-8. This article originally appeared in *Air Force* magazine.

Fozard, J.W. "Ski-Jump Jet — A Unique British Engineering Adventure", *Chartered Mechanical Engineer,* September, 1978.

Fozard, J.W. *Wind . . . Seapower . . . and Jet V/STOL,* Hawker Siddeley Aviation Ltd., August, 1976.

Gibson, Charles. "International Harrier", *Flight International,* 27 August, 1977, pp. 585-590.

Gunston, Bill. "Hawker Siddeley Harrier", a chapter from his book *Attack Aircraft of the West,* Ian Allan Ltd., London, 1974, pp. 69-107.

"Harrier into Service" *Flying Review,* September, 1969, pp. 36-41 + .

Hawker Siddeley Harrier, Famous Airplanes of the World No. 47, March, 1974, Bunrin-Do.

Horseman, Martin. *The Harrier Story,* Air Extra Number 24, August 1979.

House, D.E. and Patterson, G.A. *Carrier Suitability Evaluation of the XV-6A (P.1127) Aircraft,* NATC Technical Report FT-98R-66, 17 October, 1966.

Jackson, Jack. "Know Your AV-8 ABC's", *Product Support Digest,* McDonnell Aircraft Company, pp. 9-11.

"Kestrel Evaluation", *Flying Review International,* December, 1965, pp. 224-228.

Lindell, Clifford A. "V/STOL Design for Tactical Aircraft", *U.S. Naval Institute proceedings,* September, 1978, pp. 119-125.

MacPherson, Angus. "VIFF — The Agility Factor", *Air International,* December, 1974, pp. 263-267 + .

"Mastery in Marine Harrying", *Air Enthusiast,* February, 1973, pp. 59-62 + .

Myles, Bruce. *Jump Jet,* Presidio Press, San Rafael, CA, 1978, 265 pages.

NATOPS Flight Manual AV-8A and TAV-8A Aircraft, NAVAIR 01-AV8A-1, 1 June, 1978.

Pegasus Power — The Practical Solution to V/STOL, Rolls-Royce, Ltd., 1979.

Rowe, Charles W., Jr. "Marine Corps Harriers Make History", *Air Combat,* pp. 12-20.

Showers, Robert G. "V/STOL for Close Combat Support", *National Defense,* September-October, 1978, pp. 34-37.

Thrust Vectoring in Combat, Rolls-Royce, Ltd., October, 1978. "Tripartite VTO", *Flying Review,* Vol. 19, No. 10, pp. 15-20.

Tyler, John T. "V/STOL and the CV", *U.S. Naval Institute Proceedings,* October, 1977.

U.S. Marine Corps AV-8 V/STOL Program, Vol. III, U.S. Marine Corps.

Vectored Thrust Jet V/STOL (An evaluation of the Harrier AV-8A and the Pegasus Engine), Rolls-Royce, Ltd., December, 1978.

Vectored Thrust Jet V/STOL (Executive Summary), Rolls-Royce, Ltd., December, 1978.

V/STOL Special Report, A reprint from *Product Support Digest,* 25 May, 1977, McDonnell Douglas.

Ward, Richard L. "Hawker Siddeley Harrier'", *Aviation News,* pp. 8-9.

Warwick, Graham. "AV-8B Advanced Harrier", *Flight International,* December, 1979.

Wilmer, Graham. "Harrier Jump Jet".

Plus various issues of *Aviation Week and Space Technology,* newspaper articles and informal interviews. ■

Unusual overhead shot of VMA-231 AV-8A illustrates topside markings, flap extension, and various intake and engine compartment doors. *Rolls Royce photo*

Four 300-gallon external fuel tanks more than double the ferry range of the YAV-8B, enabling it to fly more than 2000 nautical miles. *McDonnell Douglas photo.*

Usually black and yellow, VMA-5425 saw-toothed rudder design is done here in black and grey — a sort of low visibility adaption. This AV-8A (BuNo. 158701) prepares to take off from Landing Zone Bluebird during Operation "Solid Shield", May 1976. *U.S. Marine Corps photo A453437 by A.L. Colon*

VMA-513 Harrier illustrates airplane in low visibility markings that are currently in vogue. Note that ADEN gun pods do not have ventral fins. *George Cockle photo*

Ship #6, XV-6A (A.F. serial 64-18266) hovers into landing aboard the *USS Raleigh* (LPD-1) during trials. *U.S. Navy photo PAP-26627-5-66/NATC Patuxent River*

INSIDE BACK COVER

Action onboard the *USS Guam* (LPH-9) during sea control tests. Five AV-8A's are visible in photo. Four are secured to the Guam's deck and one appears to be taxiing into position for takeoff. *Hawker Siddeley photo 741287*